American Writers Review 2022
The End or the
Beginning?

San Fedele Press

American Writers Review 2022 The End or the Beginning?

D Ferrara, Editor
Wayne Benson, Poetry Editor
Dale Louise, Copy Editor
Patricia Florio, Founder

San Fedele Press

To Those Who Find a Beginning in Every Seeming End.

Photography - D Ferrara

San Fedele Press

Contents

Photography - D Ferrara   *v*
Special Thanks to the Judges of Our 2022 Contest: *v*
A Word from the Team   *vii*
Kimberly Behre Kenna Pazienza   *1*
W. Luther Jett Zeta   *3*
W. Luther Jett Tectonics   *4*
W. Luther Jett Dark Surge   *5*
Sheree La Puma When the Children Are Buried   *7*
Sheree La Puma A Place Without Streetlights   *7*
Sheree La Puma Year of the Tiger   *8*
Emily Butler For birds it is a summer   *9*
Emily Butler If, Then   *10*
Ukraine 3/2022 - Carol MacAllister   *12*
Carol MacAllister Humanity   *13*
C.L. Liedekev Spoiler Alert   *15*
C.L. Liedekev The Prayer to my Daughter's Many Enemies   *16*
Janet Ruth Heller Leaving Our First Home   *19*
Lara Frankena Three Anesthetists   *21*
Lara Frankena Weekend Plans   *22*
Lara Frankena Newborn   *22*
Lisa Creech Bledsoe Frankie's Glass Eye   *23*
Lisa Creech Bledsoe Shades and Lights   *24*
Lisa Creech Bledsoe Wyeth's Winter Fields   *25*
Lorraine Jeffery This Afternoon   *27*
Image - Holly Tappen   *28*
Kristine Rae Anderson Transition   *29*
Kris Whorton After All   *31*
Kris Whorton Woman Reunited with Her Uterus   *32*
Kris Whorton On to Grand Isle   *33*
Photography – D Ferrara   *34*
Tricia Knoll Around My Neck   *35*
Bissera Videnova In the Small Garden A Front of the Theatre   *37*
Robert P. Arthur Clothing   *39*
Christine Gelineau Cats Can Make You Sorry   *41*
Christine Gelineau O, Lighthouse Moon   *41*

Amy Dupcak Anything Else   43
Image - Holly Tappen   44
Robin Long Amherst   45
Robin Long I watch the Ghost you wear   46
Mona Deutsch Miller My Father   49
Jonathan Lawrence What Will Happen When My World Ends?   51
Image – Carol MacAllister   52
Jean Colonomos Heaven Bound   53
John Davis Buttocks   55
Marian Willmott Hold Deep   57
G. R. Tomaini Desdemona's Secret   59
Photography - B. Carroll   60
George Looney Letter to Plumly from Erie, Late at Night   61
George Looney What It Was   62
Photography - Ana Fores Tamayo   64
Ana Fores Tamayo October 4th, for Sita   65
Lisa Delan at the end   67
Lisa Delan 3 am   68
Lisa Delan Triad   69
Paula Goldman Shoreline   71
Photography - Patricia Florio   72
Jan Elaine Harris Sea Monkeys   73
Jan Elaine Harris Invocation   74
Esther Lim Palmer First Love Formula   75
Esther Lim Palmer Cézanne's The Large Bathers   75
Mary K O'Melveny The Future of Civilization*   77
Mary K O'Melveny Confessions of a Casual Bird Watcher   79
Adam Day In Degrees   81
Photography - D Ferrara   82
Paola Caronni Walking on Water   83
Miriam Levine You Ask Yourself   85
Miriam Levine Raga   85
Miriam Levine At the End   86
Edward Wilson First Lines   87
Patricia Dutt A Better Place   89
Photography - D Ferrara   96
Jean Ende The Best Is Yet to Be   97
Ruth Ann Dandrea Snow Broke Daffodils   99

Photography – B. Carroll   *102*
Nancy Matsunaga Emergence   *103*
Dark and Light - Carol Radsprecher   *108*
Jeffrey Feingold My Left Foot   *109*
Image - Holly Tappen   *116*
Joel Savishinsky The Ghost of Schubert Walks with Me in Winter   *117*
Image - Holly Tappen   *120*
Natalie Harrison Purging Diary (kept in Google docs)   *121*
Dianne Blomberg I've Been Waiting for You   *125*
Ruth Bonapace Convulsion   *131*
Image - Carol MacAllister   *138*
Tommy Vollman Valentine Heart   *139*
Kresha Richman Warnock Jenny Moves to Albuquerque   *145*
Terry Sanville Smoke   *147*
Photoraphy - B Carroll   *152*
Pam Munter Aging Out Loud   *153*
Barry Lee Thompson Half Life   *155*
Image - Holly Tappen   *160*
Flo Golod Prudence Loses It   *161*
Pat Ryan Say Hello to Pudgy   *167*
Photography - B. Carroll   *174*
Joel Savishinsky The End Is Not Nigh   *175*
Holly Tappen Mrs. Edgewater and the Barren Orchard Trail   *177*
Mandy Pennington Save My Seat   *181*
Photography – D Ferrara   *184*
Jill Ocone Five South Thresholds   *185*
Jennifer Bryce The First Day   *187*
Christina Reiss The Way Out   *191*
Sky Rooms - John Laue   *198*
Cynthia Close The Cake Went Splat!   *199*
Photography - Patricia Florio   *202*
William Cass Happy Hour   *203*
Photography – B. Carroll   *208*
Thomas Penn Johnson Vicarage   *209*
Patty Somlo What Is Lost   *215*
Photography - D Ferrara   *220*
Burt Rashbaum What the Next Day Would Bring   *221*
Photography – B. Carroll   *224*

San Fedele Press

Don Noel Orchestral Passions 225

J. Alan Nelson Stars Die 229

Cindy Pope That Damned Blue Dress 231

Image - D Ferrara 236

Tim Walker The Ancient Widower 237

D Ferrara Arms Raised in America 239

Our Contributors 245

Special Thanks to the Judges of Our 2022 Contest:
Dawn Leas
Carol MacAllister
Vicki Mayk
Lori Myers

San Fedele Press

A Word from the Team

As we entered yet one more year of turmoil, strife, and uncertainty, we at San Fedele Press struggled with obstacles and hardships. Certainly, we were all thunderstruck by the attacks on democracy, vicious partisan splits, and violence in the United States and beyond. On a more personal level, illness, employment commitments, relocation, and family upheaval hit our small staff hard. As our submissions were soaring, and our contest attracted attention, AWR founder Pat Florio had to step away from the journal for personal reasons.

Yet, there was good news. Wayne Benson joined us as poetry editor, adding his skill to our small band. Not only did he make the submission and selection process easier and more satisfying than ever, he provided a different, welcome perspective. As a bonus, we were introduced to Wayne's entertaining and informative "Basement Poetry Podcast." Good friends Carol MacAllister, Dawn Leas, Vicki Mayk, and Lori Myers stepped in to judge our contest and offer their wisdom on the journal. Copy editor Dale Louise continues to act as the literal eyes of the journal.

In June, we hosted a lively reading and discussion, virtually. Contributors Gale Martin, Ana Fores Tomaya, and Joel Savishinsky read, followed by a discussion that ranged from humorous to profound. The participants were eager to share their experiences and, more importantly, to listen to the experiences of others.

As always, our contributors came through, offering their observations, stories, and musings. Once more, our contest entries were strong, and our regular submissions excellent. Putting together *American Writers Review* remains a privilege and a joy.

All of which has renewed our energy and broadened our horizons. In the next year, San Fedele Press will be exploring new avenues, new genres, and new distribution. You can expect more readings and more discussions, as we enjoyed in June.

While we can't predict how global conditions or political harmony will fare in the near future, we will be approaching our small corner of the literary world with fresh eyes and enthusiasm.

D Ferrara, Editor
Wayne Benson, Poetry Editor
Dale Louise, Copy Editor

Kimberly Behre Kenna
Pazienza
Co-Winner 2022 Contest

It was a simple piece of white pottery, green olive vines softening the square edges. The words, *Amarone Ristorante—Cortona, Italia*, circled around informally, in blue, as if someone had written them freehand. The four indents, one in each corner of the bowl, fit her finger perfectly. The fit felt good.

"Edward? You coming?" Vera hollered into the blank night. She tapped her cigarette into the ashtray, then let it languish in the bowl.

A dog yowled. Vera held up her empty wineglass and wiped lipstick off the rim with her thumb. She stared out at their yard where the moon caught in the teeth of dozens of dandelion leaves. Edward had chosen to ignore the pesky weeds; Vera wondered if he'd notice if she stopped giving the toilet its weekly scrub. She looked toward the house. Where was he, anyway?

Beyond their property, a streetlight sputtered on the brink of extinction. No fireflies here. In Cortona though, swarms of them would appear every night, hovering around the trellis at the end of the cypress-lined driveway. Sometimes she'd stand with him in the middle of that flickering cloud, holding hands in silence, then they'd step through the threshold, transformed, a baptism. The secluded farmhouse, meadows of sunflowers, naps in the hammock by the lemon grove. Memories tinged bright even as this mundane day melted into yesterday.

Vera turned over the ashtray and ran her finger across the name *Marco* scratched onto the bottom with something impermanent; the right side of the 'o' was nearly faded away. He'd taught her to drive a stick shift in the field behind the sheep barn. She'd stalled out, restarted, and then gunned the engine, leaving a divot.

"*Pazienza!*" He laughed, placing his tan hand on her pale knee. Patience.

Vera had fumbled and gunned again.

A cork pop transported her back to the present. Edward glugged wine into her glass till it dribbled over the rim, and she glared at the red spill seeping into the pine table.

He sat and raised his glass toward hers.

"Cheers," he said with a smile.

Vera tamped out her cigarette, and smoke tendrils snaked around the bowl of the ashtray now smudged with black ash. She stood, and without taking a breath, her unrehearsed words tumbled out.

"Edward. We need to talk."

W. Luther Jett
Zeta
Co-winner 2022 Contest

These days no sooner
are the leaves raked
than down fall more—I want
to curl up on the floor, because
the sky is the colour of November,
because this year's storms
have exhausted our alphabet,
and because if I stand
too quickly, I see
how the cliff's edge erodes.

The last train screams
before it enters the tunnel.

Trees toss frantic limbs.

We have been sent
into the Labyrinth
without a thread and if—if
we walk out and are not
devoured, it will be because

we kept one hand on the wall,
because under our breath we
kept singing, because we did not
look down though the wind
rattled dead leaves round our feet,

We followed the wind
to the end of the tunnel.

We were not captives after all.

W. Luther Jett
Tectonics

The people who walk the canyon's edge
     go down into the night
     in order to count the stars—
My blue bear watches them disappear.

A year ago, we danced in the streets
     outside the marketplace—
A bird took flight the colour of sky.

Where will you be tomorrow?
     My phone rings.
       When I pick it up
         I hear only static on the line.

Before there was a canyon there were seas,
     and seas before that,
     and before that—fire.

A song rose from the cooling rocks,
    a song which went on forever.

I uncover my face.
    The wind cools my cheeks.
        The stars open and we fall away.
            The sea rises. My blue bear waits.

W. Luther Jett
Dark Surge

This broad valley between two
ridges holds green
even when snow crusts crests
where rocks break
open—What dark surge
shakes loose eagles
from their nests, undermines
foundation-stones,
drains seas? Isn't it the same
pulse that raises
tides and mountains, guides
the stormlost petrel
home and home and home again?
Sickness pulls us
ever-widening, only to clasp
us in its grip—
Yet, we must go on, breathe
crisp air, and mark
the wend-way under one lone
star, stumble foot

and mumble song until we reach
shadows. Even then.
Until the hills descend and sea
takes all.

Sheree La Puma
When the Children Are Buried

Their under-water voices untraveled & blue
sing among roots of an Autumn Blaze
Sycamore. Fragile arms, shocks of orange,
red leaves. They crack easily at unions.
Little creatures. Spring has yet to let go its
branches. Little monster. Death rising out
of your backpack. Nineteen saplings downed
by a man that stood tall in the doorframe of
childhood. Silent in our agony, souls like
slugs feasting on poisoned milkweed. We
hear dead children sing, "who will bury you?"

Sheree La Puma
A Place Without Streetlights

Curled up in pain, I listen to waves
            withdrawing from the shoreline.
                        Black dog at my feet, whimpering.
Here I am without desire. I'm sorry
            for the thicket. Imagine the water
fat with memories, reaching
toward the mountains. High tide
this morning, everything blue.
It colors the room, my mood.

I've been in bed for 24 hours. Walls
closing in like an alley without
streetlights. There was a time
when a whiff of you could drag me
from the covers. Now I sleep
well alone. You came for
the living. I offered up penance.
How difficult it must be to love
~~me,~~ cold concrete & shame.

Sheree La Puma
Year of the Tiger

When did I ditch those hand-painted dreams?
When you showed up for dinner, I trusted no

one. Having spent my youth on a daughter, I
didn't notice the cicadas in the yard. How

they whirled off the carob tree. This new year,
this first day, I am too tired to watch clouds on

the ridge drifting towards bedlam. You who
covet bright, orange stripes remind me of

the red in me. I want to be fortified with summer.
I cannot bear another spring inert as a mannequin

in a storefront window. I want to be Maja, naked
& proud. Rip off my boots. Teach me to Samba

Emily Butler
For birds it is a summer

like any other.
Time to sing
the same songs
in the same trees.
More and more
we envy them
their ignorance.
Their peace.

Clouds marble the sky—
a drop of dye
in a tub of water.
The future isn't what it used to be.
But the sky has always looked
roughly the same.
Stable as my scent
associations. Grass
will always mean
soccer practice.
I pour coconut milk
into a pan

and suddenly
I'm at the beach,
lathering sunscreen
to protect myself
from cancer.

I'm tired of writing
about climate change
but it's like trying
not to picture an elephant
when you say "elephant."
It's like trying not to smell soccer
in cut grass.
Trying to pretend
I am a bird.

This summer it has stormed
for weeks and weeks. The earth
is angry. And yet, milk thistle
still whispers neutral truths
whenever I devote time
to an empty field.

Terence McKenna used to say,
maybe what we're experiencing
is a kind of birth—
it only looks like disaster
because it isn't finished yet.

Emily Butler
If, Then

My mind branches like fungi across the forest floor.
The forest will burn, or flood, or heal; it all depends

on which card I draw from this deck. At least
that's what I tell myself. Really, it all depends
on the choices of a couple billionaires I'll never even meet.
I am suffering.
But I still venture out to hear rain smack the street
before it washes away my house, my car, my future
in a rising panic of brown water.
I still stretch my arms towards the calm fire of our only sky.
I am lucky.
The sun is warm, but does not spark. It does us the courtesy
of not exploding. Nothing is hurtling toward the earth.
The sensation of warmth is not the sensation of burning.
It is only adjacent to, only a memory of pain.

Ukraine 3/2022 - Carol MacAllister

Carol MacAllister
Humanity

Half asleep in the evening with the TV on,
reports of war crimes are discussed.
Innocence hiding in basements,
rounded up, loaded on buses and trains.
I open the cellar door for just a moment and listen.

During the day, the TV blares WW II reruns as
I work in the kitchen. Innocence hiding in attics,
rounded up, loaded on buses and trains.
I glance up at the ceiling for just a moment and listen.

I weed out the flower beds, dead-head the roses.
A disembodied voice speaks of innocence
thrown in common graves.
I glance across the fields for just a moment and listen.

When those who come after another
thinning of our existence, and dig
up our graves feigning academic understanding,
where will I be

in catacombs under new streets,
thrown in pits of lye,
wrapped in bandages,
stuffed in a clay pot,
consumed by wastelands,
crossing the Styx to the Isle of Dead.

With so many sudden atrocities unchecked
some say there aren't enough coffins on hand.
We've used them up:

church-goers,
grocery-shoppers,
school-children,
aggressive-divisionists,
pandemic denials,
stacked in refrigerated body bags.

Extinguished innocence waiting behind
buildings to be loaded in buses and trains.
I glance them for just a moment and listen, then
close my eyes and wonder, where am I.

I lose track in the repetition of smothered humanity.
Perhaps, the concept is simply just too abstract.

C.L. Liedekev
Spoiler Alert
for Ryan Wright

After my daughter survives,
I can't find a trace of you.
No Google, no Facebook, no
updated GoFundMe
with smiles of a teenage you,
with curly hair in your face, ripped
jeans, in this picture,
you would be basking in an Ohio
sun. In mornings of rainwater,
dog shit in the grass,
and crowded high school parking lots.
But I know you are as real
as your missing form.
You are not some ghost.
You can see ghosts.

In your Make-A-Wish story,
you are in the front row,
popcorn and soda. Your
Dad points at the wrestlers
as they walk to the ring.
The crowd lost in the illusion,
their flesh of gods, Zeus
in black tights,

and Hera with hair bleached
into royalty. The illusion
will fade into a single clap.
Your dad is playing along,
knowing the champ's wink
is a slowly closing window.
The crowd subsides in a
chemical washing organs,
dulling the details.

Ryan, I can't find you. Just
those old jpegs of your hope,
the hugs you give your mother.
The bald spot of your father
matches the patch in your head.
The feeding tube in your nose,
a tired horse, run dry.
Your lips are parched; I can see
the lights dim at the corners,
the floor of the Make-A-Wish HQ,
the wrestlers with their kayfabe
smiles. Dark eyes, working hurt
night after night, hours on the road,
doctor after doctor, pills after
pills, pushing and smiling as the
wind blasts from your chest. You
have so much in common, you both
know how the match is going to end.

C.L. Liedekev
The Prayer to my Daughter's Many Enemies

It's not the bone marrow transplant you fear.
It's the days and the months after.

16

The slow limp of side effects
as they stalk up the stairwell,
invisible slashers born
of her shattered willow bones,
of her donor cell's revolt,
of broken blood vessels pouring gas into lungs.

The endless killers follow (Rhino, RSV, Adeno),
no matter their form or name, they splinter
the door in the same direction,
slitting its revenge in my skin,
the razor lettering in bold red font
is each one of her coughs
as it rushes from hallway
to stand above my bed in a murderous eclipse.

They are the shovel separating my top jaw
from bottom, greasy hands
choke me with the neck snap of guilt
and hard drawn trauma—
hard as my head through a windshield,
the slip of my desperate spit wet fingers
as the car fills up with water,
the wild dog teeth chewing my end breath.

The transplant again, its stain
drains into the basement of her helix,
and no prayer is strong enough to uproot it.
My visions are her flesh as red plumes,
a silhouette behind the blank form
of another mono killer,
its hands are all axes and viral blooms.

My mouth is the scream,
scream of no escape,

cry of not enough bleach,
not enough air purifiers, baths
or pills. And no matter what
I do she dies over and over,
video looped and looped,
the murderer has my face,
my pistol-gripped breath
garrotes her neck, rips down
into her chest, and she melts through my fingers.

Cut to the death
inside me, the legion looms—
the viral load, the immune reaction,
the mold dancing in throat and swallow,
the brain swelling pure—
all hold the handle, and choir sing
each rotation of the meat grinder
making each of my thoughts real.

Janet Ruth Heller
Leaving Our First Home

Mike and I are leaving
our first home in Sandwich, Illinois,
which we have shared for six years
since our marriage.

We have new jobs in Michigan,
but I linger in the tiny rooms
that we painted and decorated,
caress the curtains and closet hangings
that I stitched together.

The slab house is quiet,
except for the hum of the furnace,
warming us in late December.
I recall playing folksongs and klezmer music
as I cleaned or cooked or mended torn clothes.

We carry the last boxes outside,
and I sigh for our snow-covered garden,
hope the new owners will tend
the asparagus, herbs, and raspberries,
the wildflowers and magic lilies.

I look up and down Eddy Street,

already missing
the neighborhood children.
In summer, Julie and Janel
put dandelions in our mailbox,
and one Halloween, Tricia
dressed in pink taffeta
like a princess.

Mike and I load
the truck we have rented
and lock our home
for the last time.

We take the rural route east,
passing woods and cornfields.
Five white-tailed deer
bound across the road,
bidding us farewell.

Lara Frankena
Three Anesthetists

i.

I sit with a white sheet tented over raised knees, pretending to read a magazine braced against my thighs. I have an anti-Oedipal complex against the red-headed anesthetist who rests his hands on the metal rails of my gurney and asks, *You're not feeling this at all are you?* Oh, but I am. Tent, knees, magazine all collapse at the prospect of another dose.

ii.

There is no way I'm letting this bald white guy knock me out. He swipes my glasses and while I'm arguing *I want to see where I am when I wake up!* he presses a clear mask into my face—which I try to claw off. A man resembling my husband appears at the side of the gurney to distract me with a cheery *Hello!* and I pause, thinking: He's got *his* glasses...

iii.

I can't feel anything from the waist down, not even the diminutive doctor with her scalpel. It's my last chance before she slices me open; the six-foot-six anesthetist offers to brace me. We sit back to-back on the operating table. I lean into a wall of a man, and push.

Lara Frankena
Weekend Plans

My mail-order maternity frocks arrive at the office. One is white cotton, dotted with yellow flowers, the other blue satin and chiffon. Eight months pregnant, I model for my colleagues. Sales and marketing plump for slate blue. *Looks better with your trainers.*

An unexpected phone call from the Hatton Garden jeweler at 10:00 on Saturday—my ring is ready! I walk over to pick it up, then on to Covent Garden to get my face done.

Though I omit that I'm attending my own wedding when I ask the makeup artist for smokey blue eyes to match my dress, she throws in fake lashes *gratis* when I finally confess.

Lara Frankena
Newborn

Do you want to see it? Tanya whispered. As her mom sat smoking in the kitchen, we crept up to the attic to peer at her baby sister's empty crib. *Sometimes I climb in*, she said, but I wouldn't.

When my daughter is born, the midwives warn me she can die in her sleep. Then they tell me to sleep when she sleeps.

Between feeds I hover over her crib in the dark, daring myself to lay a hand on her chest. Her father snores. I should put myself to bed and hope for the best but I need to check she isn't dead yet...

Lisa Creech Bledsoe
Frankie's Glass Eye

The sun turns her wrist and light flashes in my eyes.
It is a beginning. Frankie had a glass eye
that the teacher took out daily. Maybe it wasn't every day
but it was a constant astonishment, superimposed
over preschool the way a film stutters when the strip
has too much slack, then slips and light spills everywhere.
I couldn't tell what was real and what was trick or accident,
a hidden story looping down amid spears of brilliance.
I loved the teacher, and Frankie. I loved Frankie's glass eye.

In my childhood memory, Frankie's eye rolled
across the linoleum when the teacher slipped
and dropped it. And I was watching Frankie watching
it roll with his pink astonished socket.
What I wanted to see was the magic
behind my friend's thin, fringed curtain. It was
Frankie magic, eye magic, maybe my magic with Frankie
laying with his head in her lap and the windows behind
rejoicing in lit hallelujahs, saving me,
saving all of us up in the miracle.

It wasn't round, the glass eye. It wasn't even
glass. I dreamed of deft small cups brimming
with what Frankie and I couldn't see. I didn't need
eyes for a holy light-drenched classroom filled with

Horton and Harold and *Are You My Mother*. Those were
wing-beating in the light, transferred by breath, magnificent
and mundane. I wanted eyes for behind our house at night
where the streetlights built black, absent shadowhouses
that stretched and loped along our street, greedy and famished.
I needed to see what might escape in the alarming sound at the end
of Peter and the Wolf before you could get the needle off the record.
Frankie's eye knew what was in the sidewalk cracks and whether
our mothers were fragile or doomed. I bowed before the eye, kept
clean hands and never spoke of any of the secrets seen
in the preschool pietà, the calm knowing of what lay ungently
on the other side.

Lisa Creech Bledsoe
Shades and Lights

I'm walking toward the center but
not the one you're thinking. There are
two cups for the offering: one full, the other
anxious. Supply lines are not
to be relied upon in the same way
the yellow leaves of a spiceberry tree
drift in the understory like fireflies
under the blackwhite sky. Which

light to follow, or which shade?
Only yesterday I thought of anything
I wanted, and it grew wings
and sailed across the world to find me
today. That only happens for some of us
and extracts a cost we barely understand.
My idle thoughts are carved on someone
else's scar-hashed skin.

I fill the hollow chambers
of a buckeye husk—
      first offering
with late haws—
      second offering. Now
small red stars mark the location
of at least one holy sadness.

Yesterday I carried today's date
written on paper to every place
on the mountain but didn't know
what to ask. God only knows
what is buried here, what golems
still walk, and whether
their arms are filled with knives
or clocks or bees.

Lisa Creech Bledsoe
Wyeth's Winter Fields

Yesterday our neighbor shot a buck who managed
to bolt to our side of the mountain before dying.
Three hours later he halloo'd us, dragging the deer
down to our gravel drive. It will take him two days
to process it. They will have meat to get them
through this winter and next spring.

My adult son did the dishes last night in one of his
many all-night vigils. This morning I woke to a clean
kitchen, and made us both breakfast before he went to bed.
Then I sat down at my computer to research the connection
between amphetamines and facial tics. Sometimes this helps.

I let my house get much dirtier now than I once did,

though we no longer have three small boys—
their friends and sticks and projects everywhere.
My girlfriend from those years had a handwritten note
in her kitchen that said "Someday my house will be clean."
Now I try not to think what that actually means.

Today I walk on the mountain to gather what few greens
the winter shares. My dog is excited by the bloodstains
on the drive, the scent of deer. The earth and I turn
toward our bones where hidden suns wait.

Lorraine Jeffery
This Afternoon
(A haibun)

Ash hangs heavy, as smoke from seven hundred miles away clogs my valley. My sore throat announces the haze before it blurs the rocky outlines of closeup mountains. Three million acres in California, one million in Oregon. Western states burning.

> plumes of memories
> flow east, and catch
> on jagged peaks

Only charred beams and ashes in the towns of Paradise, California and Talent, Oregon. The comfort of walled safely is lost forever and even precious spring rain, if it comes at all, warns of unchecked flooding. Legions of firefighters come but the hills still blaze.

> birds vanish
> nightly jewels glow
> spring rains gouge

Today, I see billows of smoke from my front window—flames on my mountains, as plane after plane dumps. I stare at the pictures, journals, keepsakes, and books that wouldn't fit into my packed car.

> trees torch
> my burning world
> hot wind chokes

Image - Holly Tappen

Kristine Rae Anderson
Transition

If a wildfire tore
toward our neighborhood
and we had time just
to grab the dog, all
three legs of him, and
maybe two armloads
of boxes to fling
into the back seat
of the Prius and
go before streets clogged
like catastrophic
five o'clock traffic

because we'd be forced
to abandon some
things—most things—to weigh
our favorite treasures
(signed first editions,
high school yearbooks, my
father's World War II
discharge papers, our
son's scuffed baby shoes,
bound notebook-journals,
our lifetimes of words),

so standing at the
car, hesitating
only a beat, one
of us will say, "Hon,
they're just *things*, you know,"
and the other will
nod, achingly, as
we both click open
our car doors, tumble
in with the dog, take
one conclusive look
as the car backs from
the driveway and we
shift into forward.

Kris Whorton
After All

Grace's ashes reside in a thimble-sized container
inside a small covered trinket dish.
She wanted to be broadcast
in a place she'd never been
or a place she loved. Now
she is tucked away like the tiniest
Matrushka doll. Setting her alight
makes my heart clench.
Some parts will land, others
will find leaf tops, riverbeds. Some will drift
to space. To that place of no sound.
No light between stars and planets.
Vastness too large for my brain.
Sending her into nothingness
scares me.
Ending up as nothingness

scares me. All of my parts alight,
miniscule particles of brain and bone
that could be spread across a glacier.
No body to mourn. No
sure place forever; once a glacier,
a lake, then rain, mist, air.

Instead of cremation, I want to be
the person found in the snowbank, parka
unzipped, eyes closed and face
peaceful. Or better yet, smiling.
There on a mountainside,
Everest say, or somewhere in Antarctica,
Siberia, even Pluto if I could travel all
those miles or lightyears before death
came to me. Before nothing
becomes nothingness
forever.

Kris Whorton
Woman Reunited with Her Uterus

Some odd things: a goat wearing a necklace, a teacup carrying
astronaut tethered as he roams outside the shuttle, a dog

driving a limousine through the narrow streets of Lisbon. Odder
still: the man, your doctor, standing in front of your spread legs,

your feet in stirrups, paper towel blanket covering your exposed
parts as he talks about the vaccination, gas prices, how hot it's been

these last weeks. You want to say, *Get on with it already. It's not
like you're interviewing for a job.* He tells you everything looks

normal and you remember 7th grade biology, your teacher showing
the class a fist-sized burgundy Bosc pear, holding the fat end

up. *This is your uterus*, he said, and the boys looked at the girls.
The girls felt the future, and past perhaps, of legs spread

in front of boys men they barely knew and never wanted to open for
in any way. What a mystery life is when you die a little

a thousand ways, day after day, and no one hears you.

Kris Whorton
On to Grand Isle

My husband at home, me no longer living with him
but married still. Divorce papers, signed by me

part of the gulf between us. Another gulf,
3 or 4 states, separate us as does the man

I'm traveling with. After a few hours walking
in New Orleans, we're harried by the too loud,

too stifling, too busy for this weekend
we've cut out of our lives. On a road south

lined by water, marsh grasses
stand bright green against a hazy sky.

Stilt houses rise alone or in pairs on vast
stretches of space and time. The end

of the road a barrier of land between land
sea and more sea. Walkways raised

above sand, beaches separated from roads
by dune grasses, birds alight, their cries,

frenzied flight, the only company we seek.

Photography – D Ferrara

Tricia Knoll
Around My Neck
After Samuel Taylor Coleridge, *The Rhyme of the Ancient Mariner*

The sky goes hot and copper
over sunset hills on fire.
     My friend's house burned
     in Sonoma. To scorched ground.
All-around ice that flowed before is no more.
     I went to Mendenhall to say I once knew
     ice squeezed blue.
Slimy things that crawl go few.
     You know they do.

Cast-offs foul every sea painted in oil slicks.
     I went to Manzanita Beach with a kitchen sieve
     and sorted bits of plastic and broken bottles
     beside children in green t-shirts
     dragging garbage bags.

I walk a lonesome road with you. And you. And you.
     We fail to see what follows.
     The young in green t-shirts.
     Ghosts of slimy things that used to crawl.
     Fiends stirring silence when we did not listen

to ghastly tales we must repeat for babes
in green. Drought. Ocean circulation slowing.
Carbon hung in sky. The whale's cry.

A dead white bird hangs around my neck. And yours.
The spell has snapped.
Stop the bridal guest. Yell at the senator.
Mend the wind-ripped flag.
Where we have been alone
on the wide, wide sea,
raise a hand within the tide.

Bissera Videnova
In the Small Garden A Front of the Theatre
(before the social distance)

It was easy
because everything was in its place:
the check players in front of the stone table
for a game of emotional oppression
the trickles of water
were going back into the pool,
from where they would squeeze through
the narrow drain—
the tunnel, in which treacherous
the hollow guts would rumble
before they got enough
of the evening and daily town's romance.
It was easy.
The growing ecology
proved by the number of birds
collected the sound of kisses
which passes through by force
and sewed the mouth of the children's hubbub.
It was easy.
Cracked popcorn—
a ballerina with a wad
danced her fair well without a swan
on the stage, she improvised quickly—

a pool of spilled beer on the flagging
the violets—orderly,
the musicians—untidy,
the photos of the sequential biennale—
befittingly respected.
It was easy.
The chaplin's kid
would go around with the sling
at the opening of the season.
In the climax, there will be other slings as thongs——
these, hidden in the semi-spheres of gentle hemispheres;
It was easy.
The trees agreed finally,
to dress.
The thirsty people were thirsty.
The drunks were drunk.
In April.

Robert P. Arthur
Clothing

My closet door is mine to open, but not captive really
Behind it my jackets whisper

(some may be whispering)

Who will be chosen?

Four black jackets and matching pants await a funeral
I am terrified. My future's behind me, damn me

damn you damn me
(maybe some are whispering, maybe not)

The brown herringbone tweed is swinging from the rack,
losing control

(I've known jackets to not give a buck) (What hanging's
desirable)

I am lying in my bed, thinking of she whom I've lost,
my meds beside me. The red ring on my finger is turning on and off
in the dark

(speaking up, maybe not)

In spite of the music, my white dinner jacket may be suicidal

She whom I've lost makes a winding sheet of my coat of gray linen
that holds her in its arms

(our aroma surrounds us, damn us)

My other coats are the cruelest of all

The sea blue coat drops too deep
The sky blue coat ascends too far

Christine Gelineau
Cats Can Make You Sorry

Cats can make you sorry
you ever fed them,
or caressed their sleek fur
or spent time thinking up
a sweet name to call them.
You're shrieking that name now
in a frantic duet with
the goldfinch's desperate death cries.
The cat eyes you with disdain.
You're close enough to witness
the Caligulan sport, how he sets her down
backs up–the showman's touch
to this display of prowess. He waits.
She waits.   In a spasm of hope
the finch opens her wings, the flutter,
the liquid pounce, the dark act
in its reiterating encore.

Christine Gelineau
O, Lighthouse Moon

O, lighthouse moon,
throughout the snow-blanketed night,
you turn the dull disc of your face

upon us and beam reflected radiance
in translucent shafts like the rays
of divine light in the illustrations
of a children's bible—a phenomenon
officially known as refraction, yet
even knowing the optical effect
is luster bent by ice crystals in the air
does not expunge my impression
of a waterfall of light bridging
from the moon to the meadow
outside my window as if,
while the human world sleeps,
our battered earth, in silver silence,
is being transfused with exactly
the holy reverence due her.

Amy Dupcak
Anything Else

I came out singing the wrong kind of song,
not a song of myself but a song that longs

to be anything else. I clung to the darkness as long
as I could, then broke my mother in two, sent her

bleeding into an operating room. I waited alone,
alive. Eight years before, my mother flatlined

on a different hospital bed, writhing like a fish
caught in a net, the thread of her soul

coming loose. A priest had tried to give her
Last Rites, but she'd screamed delirious.

Was she possessed? Was I? Before my birth
I was an electric spark that lit the sky,

a guttural roar that broke the earth, a speck of
dark matter drifting along—the song before the song.

All of that gone the moment my mother wrestled me out.

Image - Holly Tappen

Robin Long
Amherst

I wonder often
if through once-photographed-fields and rolling wheels—
the radio gone silent
for the sound of scratching pavement narration—

if *Recollection* finds—

and becomes a tumbling column,
a soft tornado,
flinching with our papered decay
that sooner dies away at deciphering,
entering,
touching the spin—
Remorse's fingertip whim, you might imagine.

but there is no eye left to reach,
relive,
redo—
no sacred space saved in the gliding chaos
we created— unaware —
so you straighten your back—steer—
steady,
as the white lines tick past
and the upturned dust floats in your wake—
suspended,

safe,
there—in your mirror's reflection—

where it will be captured,
gathered,
packed and pressed
to the earth again.

Robin Long
I watch the Ghost you wear

I watch the Ghost you wear—
shift
by days, seasons, moods—
as though the absence of the words at close
liberated
every language after.

Mid-twilight? Martyr—
crouched before a hologram altar
in sheets of conviction,
hushing forlorn missives to me in whispers,
at rope's end, dragged on,
as nails drive furrows in the earth—
eyes gone wide with the sky
of some horizon—
realized,
I might hope.

Some dusks—
Saboteur—
when your face gives shape to the echoes.
Critiques—release—spring from your lips
at phrases on pages still

helpless,
unfinished—
yet midnights,
I see more tenderly
in image—a Kinsman.
A doting pair of hands,
cradling a cover,
laying in a grass I never knew

.

In morning, an Artist, urging
a song of sweet force:
Don't forget to write,
you insist

Don't

forget

to write.

Messy, kind—soon, only
unscripted quiet,
numbed—I imagined at the time—
in costumed premonition.

Other hours? Villain—
hurling subsistence
into the hollows of a spine,
where seamed, I bleed the same ink
that never could convince

the story—itself—was sound.

Other moments,
a Stranger. But

Strangers do not mourn,
she said—Dickinson—
in *the Heart I former wore*

so, I envision instead, *Familiar,*
in pieces of panes meeting
at the obscured glass's center—
a knuckle,
merely hovering, tempered,
as the years turn away.

Citations:
Emily Dickinson, F756A "Bereavement in their death to feel"
Emily Dickinson, F757A, "I think To Live—may be a Bliss"

Mona Deutsch Miller
My Father

My father was a bull in a china shop
He saw himself caught in the ring
The circle closing in. He smashed
and gnashed and bashed our mother,
and dug his words, like horns, into us

He wanted to lead a charge,
Up and away to open country,
Golden hills and bare trees, like Texas,
But ended up in Manhattan,
Jostling against that "surly bunch" on the IRT.

The ground we covered was hot or icy,
His pat on my head turned into a cuff
His kindness inchoate and hidden.

He made Beef Wellington but wouldn't follow
the directions for Jell-o. He refused to look
up movie times, so we missed the beginnings.

But we made a full circle, Daddy and I—
The girl who wouldn't kiss him on her wedding day,
The one who dreamed of escaping him.
At least we got to see the endings twice
And our second ending was a good one.

Jonathan Lawrence
What Will Happen When My World Ends?

Will vampires hang on street lights baring fangs?
Will men and women marinate steak in plastic bags,
fry spuds in trash can fires?
Will children bounce cadences on
waterlogged mattresses, sinking teeth
into meat and starch making bloody mush,
giggling while they show it?
When night falls and it's only bats opening wings
like doorways, wrapping dark
down to my bones.
Will everyone be having fun
when I'm on the couch salivating?
I'm the King of bathroom breaks,
Sultan of few words and no thoughts,
Magnate of escapism. Don't get me
too close to the hard stuff or you'll
have more than a revelation on your hands.

Image – Carol MacAllister

Jean Colonomos
Heaven Bound

You were my dream catcher, Mom,
my desire to study dance caught
in your 3rd-eye's web. At eight years -old
you knew to take me to Ballet Arts in Manhattan,
a serious dance studio where kids and
professional ballerinas trained.

Some teachers were Russian émigrés from
Sergei Diaghilev's *sensationel* Ballet Russe
when in early 1900 Vaslav Nijinsky
astonished Paris and the West.
>   His *entrechat dix* was a vertical jump
>   where he crossed his legs ten times
>   while airborne.

>   Heaven bound, why would he come down?

Many company members emigrated to New York.
Their shaman's knowledge of grace harked back
two centuries to court dances from Peter the Great's reign.
George Balanchine was another import. He believed
>   *You put a group of men onstage, you have a group of men.*
>   *You put a group of women onstage, you have the world.*

I wanted to be part of that world, I wanted to
      reach transcendence through physical extremes,
what Mr. B. believed.

My first important teacher, Madame Vera Nemchinova,
would crack her cane against the wood barre
and yell, *I VAS BOLSHOI,* as if
our Raggedy Anne bodies were insults.
The wood barre shook with her past glory and I'd work harder
      to suck in my belly, or from a standing position, I'd cramp
      my over arched foot when I slid it to the side in *tendu.*
Madame sometimes recognized my efforts and would wink,
whooshing a tempered joy through my body.

Oh Mom, the day of remembrance
is the day you led me to Ballet Arts
where the dream you caught landed at the ballet barre.
Thank you for sending me through doors
that opened the rest of my life.

John Davis
Buttocks

A behind or bum—we all have one
rear stub rump
two half-moons, beautiful moons

Where does *butt ugly*
get its ugly—not from the curves
or the smooth skin, not from
the tooshie cushion or the bump
it bumps against doing the bump

Derriere feels so French
You sip a white Bordeaux
Derriere naughty, good naughty,
lace naughty in a boudoir

Keister, tush, tail, can,
always there's an ass which flattens
romance—think jackass,
stomping donkey, kicking trashcans

But imagine buns, warm buns,
dinner rolls by Fanny
that have held you all day
at a desk or driving miles
over back roads while a truck
grinds gears

Bless the bottom, the stern,
the smooth end
Any backside booty
anytime feels fine

Marian Willmott
Hold Deep

Not a word.
A thick fog hangs
over the deserted beach.

Dead minnows
abandoned by tide's surge
stink in tangles of seaweed.

My heart knows
the cold stone of loss,
the silence of time.

The weight of each step
molds wet sand, leaving
a constellation of my passing.

I put the perfect spiral
of a snail shell in my pocket.
A gull dips and soars—

there is no horizon,
no beginning or end.
My skin is salt spray and wind.

Thoughts and worries
dissolve, giving way
to surf's rhythmic insistence.

My driftwood bones
hold deep
the wings of this day.

G. R. Tomaini
Desdemona's Secret[*]

Iago my soul , never can we be together !

Take my hand , as I pour out my heart :

I cannot love that brute ! *My life is over* .

You must greet me in the Elysian Fields^{**}. . .

only then may we be together ! Until then :

stir up Othello ' s temper : *push him to the deed* ;

do you really think I can live without you in my

arms , Iago ? *Go forth and implement my will !*

Desdemona , how I am your vassal ! *So mote it be !*

———————————————

*Shakespeare, William—*Othello*
**Carlos Schwabe—*Elysian Fields*

Photography - B. Carroll

George Looney
Letter to Plumly from Erie, Late at Night
after Richard Hugo

I remember years ago introducing you, Stanley, to my friend
Doug, both of you gone now. It was a writers' conference.
You had a drink in your gnarled hand and a young woman
close beside you with that look women can get
that can only be adoration tinged with a calming sorrow,
a recognition of what age does to us. Memory fails me,
as they say, so I think of you both sitting somewhere
indescribable, drinking, a half-empty bottle on the table.
Dead, my friend feels free to drink again, addiction a worry
only the living have. Hummer once wrote of "a language
so pure it would require / no mind to contain it, no voice
to speak it, no body / to breathe it out of its own air into
its own air." That's the language the two of you, half-drunk
and dead long enough you've both gotten past any denial
of being dead, whisper to one another as though not wanting
to be overheard, as if what you have to say is meant to be
said to no one else. Certainly not anyone still aware of a body
more and more a catalog of subtle and not-so-subtle pain.
Not someone who might wake to the concerto of wrens
shivering the stunted maple and want to make up lyrics
to sing to that morning music. The same way I made up
the two of you being together in some obscure local bar,
sipping twelve-year-old Tullamore Dew and talking
about something that, not being dead, I can't understand

even the language in which you're discussing whatever it is
I'd need to have given up the subtle music of those wrens
and the sorrow of a beautiful woman to even begin to be
able to imagine, much less to have a thing to say about it
that would be worth the saying. Except maybe to say
the woman comes back from somewhere she's been to
that table in the tavern where the dead come to drink
and keep each other from being completely alone
and gives each of you a peck on the cheek before asking
one of you to dance as Van Morrison's "Moon Dance"
starts up from the old-fashioned jukebox in the corner
and the two of you smile and both of you rise and take,
each of you, one of her hands and the three of you step out
onto what passes for this bar's dance floor and her
blond hair in the dim light is something a wren would
have to come up with a new song for and the anything
but calm scent of her pheromones makes you both believe
death could be something you could dance your way out of
if only she were to stay in your arms as the music makes you
remember what it meant to have a body and to be
in love with what Hugo coined the hurt world worth having.

George Looney
What It Was

Not what you would call an expression
of grace, this grey sky diffused by the drift

down of what some might say is a dusting
of snow. Which of course is for the most part

silent, which means I'd hear what you might say
if your tongue were not ash in some urn

in a state south of here where any snow
would be a reason to call everything off.

Not the sky again, you say. Isn't it time
you let go of the Romantic tic

of examining the world for some hint
of what you'd say is meaning? And I can't

argue with you, though this drifting snow might
have a say as to how to reconcile

the contradiction between what we call
grace and what we think of as loss. Enough

has come down already everything is
lost to what it was. We like to say this

is wisdom, this white that makes everything
a ghost. We say it's change. It is loss.

Photography - Ana Fores Tamayo

Ana Fores Tamayo
October 4th, for Sita

This day for eight years now
has brought to me an overwhelming sadness
that catapults me from sound slumber
to remind me that life is ever ephemeral,
not lasting eons,
and what we now have is borrowed though much loved.

Like my mother's caring touch eight years ago
left me on this fourth day in October filled with autumn day and
       falling leaves,
eight years later to the day
my bloodhound,
my boon companion, my friend my love,
sauntered a goodbye gone forever now.

My gentle giant used to slumber
by my side while I wrote my essays,
while I cried my woes,
while I championed folks in need of help,
while I cried in pain for others and for me.
And she looked to me,
placing her soft nozzle on my lap,
kissing me when she thought I needed it,
tenderly muzzling the lobe of my left ear
to let me know everything would be alright.

But now she's left me,
just as softly as she came into my life,
just as regally as she would wrap me in her gaze,
her large brown eyes'
bloodhound look of knowledge
queenly drooping ears
flopping all her wisdom,
assuring me that I could get through just another day...

What will I do without you?

She's smelled the yucca sauntering up, though,
the garden path to where my mother waits for her
upon her day, eight years ago, October 4th.
And she has left me, to join my mother now, on this *their* day.

Lisa Delan
at the end

> You kill her slowly,
> suddenly
> your scythe tenderly
> attuned to all the
> soft places where
> you lived when
>   *you loved her.*
>
> You excise her faith,
> milk her breasts
> and bury her spine
> by the tree in
> the yard where
> you carved that
>   *you love her.*
>
> Her eyes scooped,
> by talons dropped
> in a field where they
> are now cornflowers
> staring at the sun -
> and oh, how
>   it loves her.

So you burn her hair,
inhale the silt
and fill your jaws
with all that was;
with all the worlds
you lost in
 loving her.

Lisa Delan
3 am

i am afraid
no one will
see me drown

when the brack
swells rise and
wrap my heels

and my breath
buried under
green glass

eyes gritted
open to swallow
the storm

weighting my
body as
i roll under

dragging the
bottom until
light filtrates

far away in
a dream of
rising

i open my mouth
and all the sea
rushes out

Lisa Delan
Triad

I came into your joy
and fell upon the lap of grace,
a whirling dervish in
a dance of revelation,
the three of us twirling
entwined and free and
wrapped in the sheen
of promise.

We were upswept in
ecstatic devotion,
turning in time together-
meeting the mystic
with eyes, minds
open and sinewed,
embracing earth and above,
the music of the spheres.

But then we looked down,
lost under our feet-
struggling to balance as
flutes and hymns dimmed;

dizzy and pallid we
dropped on our cloaks,
far from the sama
and further from home.

How many times did we
dance, ascend, and fall?
I cannot count;
and still we spun
courting the divine,
hands met in prayer
for all we would hold
if we had looked up.

Paula Goldman
Shoreline

As the water flowed over our touching
feet, steadily sinking, and the tide pulling out,
my soles rooted in the sand, to all
around me: you, your silly long-sleeved blue shirt,
the midday's bright sky, the running shoreline
where the water comes to call us home. Opening
to you as the sea opens, endlessly
returning to sweep the beach, then receding: we
could never last, you were a poem even then.

Photography - Patricia Florio

Jan Elaine Harris
Sea Monkeys

when the sea monkeys die all at once
their carcasses rise to the tank's lid

one hundred cellophane husks
get poured out in the alley

we sterilize the empty tank
scrub the residue from its sides

once we can stabilize the environment
we'll order more creatures

we are certain future specimens
will close the unending loop

and when our new package arrives
we double check the tank's PH levels

we hold our breath as 100
        unhatched bodies thud when

they hit the water and
 sink beneath its surface

every body a rigid parable
a koan in free fall

between mortality and disposal
guilelessness and rebirth

Jan Elaine Harris
Invocation

pink dawn recalls our hominid
ancestors who stood on plateaus
their lips broken by whispers
their bodies open to the same sun
cresting over the horizon
**

they did not learn about stars
they could not imagine an astral furnace
for them no divination no priestcraft
no augury no urge to sacrifice
these bipedal bands wobbly
naked moving forward
through 1.2 million years
of darkness and day
**

language sleeps inside them
myths and tales are unimaginable
instead they listen for birdsong
and respond by standing up
happy to straighten their spines
and welcome a little more light.

Esther Lim Palmer
First Love Formula

> Everyone's had a first love.
> And many
> An accompanying theory
> Of what went terribly wrong.
> What do you call a theory
> That can't be tested? Proof
> That not all can be reduced
> To science. You loved
> Telling me that sometimes, there is
> No why. But always a how.
> Like how you met X.
> Like how you did Y.
> And when I couldn't take you back,
> How you dared to ask me why.

Esther Lim Palmer
Cézanne's The Large Bathers

> Brave are those moments he chose to leave
> Blank. Lines of translucent light, we learn
>
> To hide and render opaque.
> For isn't that how we survive? Still,

There is no Titian chiaroscuro here.
Those luscious days are gone.

We are two-dimensional now.
Plastic parts, deconstructed

And exposed. Ugly and unsensual.
At least the triangle remains: Hope

Of a unifying dream?
Or perhaps another act

To frame our barren condition—
A lone man

Walking away in search of a god,
Accompanied only by horse and poverty.

Mary K O'Melveny
*The Future of Civilization**

There are twenty polar bears.
Their ivory coats cast a luminescent
glow against gunmetal grey skies,
seaweed-toned mists and volcanic
rock formations with a mica sheen.
Some bears peer out from behind
the weather station's glassless windows,
as if they are about to welcome
guests for late afternoon tea.

Others wander past rusted canisters,
dismantled iron pipes which lie in heaps
like broken children's toys. Skeletons
of windmill towers dot the landscape.
The drone camera hovers overhead.

---

* Dimitry Kokh, a Russian photographer, used a low-noise drone
to photograph polar bears on Wrangel Island in Kolyuchin, near
the northern coast of Chukotka in the Russian Federation. The
bears live in buildings that once housed a weather station. Built
in the 1930s, the station was abandoned in 1992. Wrangel Island
is a UNESCO-designated nature preserve and refuge.

It has been specially designed
to photograph quietly, like some
Cold War spy, huddled behind
an indistinct black Nash Rambler.
The aging fortress, abandoned
thirty years ago by Russian scientists,
seems well suited to its new denizens.
Its structures have stayed mostly upright,
wooded roof slats still in place, copper
chimney pipes aimed at the heavens.
Flashes of ochre, lemon yellow
and pale blue paint blend on exterior
walls, like chiaroscuro woodcuts.

The bears are relaxed, curious as cats.
A few stroll about on neon green
mossy ground. One imagines
how they might sink down into
its spongey surface, each footstep
leaving behind a webbed pawprint
large as a cast iron frying pan.

When sunshine licks away thick fog,
the bears posture themselves like
Mediterranean sunbathers. One can
almost see them smile as they loll
on the hillside, watching the Arctic
Ocean transform to ribbons of lapis lazuli
as sunshine emerges like an eager child.
Careful eyes keep tabs on swimming seals.

The photographs remind me
of the ubiquitous sheep that dot
Ireland's hillsides bordered by shades
of green, ancient stone mounds, an
endless sea. Lately, our thoughts of
polar bears tend to be Shakespearean:
a cruel hunger slimming them down
to bone, eyes gazing without seeing,
as they drift on melting floes of ice.

But these bears have merrier tales to tell.
On this island refuge, danger has receded.
Human calamities have no place here
where wooly mammoths once roamed.
Our alabaster mammals swim, dive, romp
and range free as ivory gulls. Staring at
the drone, they seem to saying to us: *Move
out. Move on. We are doing great without you.*

Mary K O'Melveny
Confessions of a Casual Bird Watcher

This late October morning, I ventured out for a walk
along our creek where rose pink golden leaves saw
their future selves twisting and bobbing, pierced in halves
and quarters like scattered coins. The day began raw,
the way late fall can evoke a tear, like dew or a
lamentation. I passed through fronds of grass
once home to purple martins feasting on a wall
of milkweed. I moved aside to let our old tortoise pass
(he's lived here longer than me) and sensed his eyes
were also clouded by sadness. Above, geese headed abroad
following ancestral cartography. I wondered if they thought
about how earth transforms each year or just flew ahead,

unquestioning, into thinning layers of blue. No one is cautious
enough these days, especially birds. Habitats thin, each crumb
powders, drifts off—dispersed like a billion feathers
silenced. Songbirds of every octave were once at home
here. Now, they are faint memories bleached bone white as ocean
reefs. Sequoias, rubberwoods, kapoks have formed a jagged seam
across the planet, no longer able to offer shade from a hot noon
sun. I want to join the leaves in my creek for a swim.

Adam Day
In Degrees

A window is not
a wall, but both

are empty. It's just
this, as it is. Slow

rain in alders. Hard
to tell if the tree

is holding up
the house or

the house, the tree.

Photography - D Ferrara

Paola Caronni
Walking on Water

Wouldn't it be good

to walk on water
alone,
feet grazed by the waves,
tickled by the bites
of nosy fish.

To leave behind
little fires on the beach,
crab carcasses, pebbles,
plastic bottles, bright buoys.

You could glide for miles on the
same sheet of water,
only its colour changing
according to the depths of oceans,
the moods of the sky.

Passing countries like floating bodies,
it all looks peaceful from there,
the occasional warship
in wait.

You hop islands. It's not

where you want to settle.
You already feel like one.
Island.

Nobody kicks you out of its
territorial waters
for not wearing a mask,
not filling in forms,
nor getting tested.

With reverence, someone
rolls down a red carpet of neatly knitted
purple sea-moss,
enticing you to land.

And you can reach
your family
shore,
a lighthouse on a rock,
                its light off.

You knock at the door
dressed in barnacles, encrusted mussels.
Your mojos are a sea urchin, a shark tooth you hang
to the naked tree.

They let you in, hug your scraggy body,
touch your salt-wrinkled face.
They see themselves reflected
in your vagrant eyes.

You're unsullied, clean,
      you're there, for them.
You've stepped off the horizon,
you've walked miles and miles
            on water.

Miriam Levine
You Ask Yourself

Near that house with the green door, you ask yourself,
What would it be like to be a different person,
contented to cook a meal and mend a tear
and live in that house and not be driven?

You think it may be time to leave your old self,
not like the Carmelites who take a vow of silence,
a new name and pray day and night for the world,
but something like them, someone who speaks less.

Miriam Levine
Raga

Let me imagine we come again
to the great hall to hear the master.
We're all ages and purged of regret.
We do not think of the past or lust
for food or worry about our looks.
The master plays on endlessly,
notes falling like a shower of seeds,
the summer a distinct season once again.
Fires have stopped burning, seas recede,
the precious sky at last an infinite blue.

Miriam Levine
At the End

At the end of summer when nights turn cold
he would sleep alone in the small downstairs room
with the low window open so he would hear
the crickets' throb and feel the dark roll over the sill.
The wind sent a leafy branch against the clapboards.
Beyond the black oaks the moon rose and his heart
beat to the rhythm of the crickets that seemed never to end.

Edward Wilson
First Lines
with respects to Bulwer-Lytton

- Under the streetlight, the asphalt was gleaming in the rain, slick as a load of oil from a mangled tanker, but not as slick as the one she'd put over on me.

- I'd sworn to quit, but when I lit the last one with my scarred Zippo, it dropped from my lips like a monk to his knees in front of a saint at what I saw in the quick flash.

- He'd been in my shop before, but never with anything to pawn. He set the box between us on the counter
  "You sure you want to do this?" I asked.
  With a shaky hand he drew it back and, after a moment, pushed it toward me again.
  "Here's what happened," he said.

- I liked the room. It was a place I could live. But whoever had just slammed the door and locked it behind me figured my life would be as short as an international call with a cheap phone card.

- I don't like reunions. But when I turned through the dusty yearbook I'd unpacked and saw that face, I called and made the reservation

San Fedele Press

- Scotch is my drink. Straight up if the bottle has a cork. Anything else, on the rocks with water on the side. Until I pushed through the door with the lion's head knocker and walked into that bar.

- The chair had sat in that corner for more than 60 years—doing its duty, not knowing or caring who sat. The man in it now didn't know or care either. He was beyond that.

- I'm a married man—two kids, a wife, a house in the suburbs. I've worked hard for those promotions. Still, at the office, I couldn't help glancing at her from time to time, but nothing more. This morning, in the men's room, when I opened the note she'd dropped on my desk as she swayed by, there was an address and a time—7:00pm.

- When I picked the lock and opened the apartment door, a plate and a cup were drying in the rack by the sink. The plants looked healthy and a well-fed fish watched me from his tank. But the closet was empty and the dresser drawers. I was late again, as I had been too many times in the past seven years. It was getting to be a habit and one I swore I'd break.

- With an arm against the wall, Carson braced himself and eased gingerly into the dim room. Until now he had not realized how slick blood could be. And there was plenty of it.

- The parrot saw everything, but he wasn't talking.

Patricia Dutt
A Better Place

Ally gently opened Mrs. Bunker's front door. The door was never locked in case Mrs. Bunker needed to make a fast exit. "Hello Mrs. Bunker!" Ally called. "It's Tuesday and I'm here. It's me! Ally-Allison!"

Ally waited at the doorway, preferring to enter with permission because startling the frail Mrs. Bunker could cause a heart attack or other calamity. Gurgling erupted from the condo's back bedroom so she dropped her cleaning supplies and ran, sandy sneakers on the cream-colored rug. There was Mrs. Bunker: flat on her back, a whale of a woman contentedly snoring away.

"Mrs. Bunker," Ally said louder. A ghoul on TV was doing the death rattle again and again, but previous messing with the volume had caused Mrs. Bunker to shoot upright as if a tight spring had been sprung.

On the floor next to the bed was her junky Dollar Store purse, open wide, her wallet of credit cards visible: easy picking for sticky fingers. Anyone could tiptoe in and rob the poor woman blind. Sometimes Mrs. Bunker was awake when Ally made her entrance. She'd wait for special instructions while Mrs. Bunker would be singing along (or trying to) to the religious shows. The preachers praying, singing, lecturing, chastising: *It's like a rerun of my marriage*, she jokingly told Ally, and how could Ally not love the elderly woman? Then Mrs. Bunker would motion with her hand—come on Ally-Allison. Ally would sing along, but not for long because she had work to do.

"Yoo-hoo, Mrs. Bunker! It's Tuesday. Laundry day!"

Mrs. Bunker licked her lips. She was nearly 90, but Ally preferred Mrs. Bunker to other clients whose cultural biases wrapped around their brain like a layer of plastic wrap that could suddenly shrink and tighten. It was invisible to them but Ally felt it in her gut. Was it worth the bad feelings and potential job losses to enlighten them? That was being judgmental, wasn't it? Imposing her views on them?

Ally was biracial and depending on the light, and to most people, she could be Black or White. Her mom would say: *Damned if you do and damned if you don't, Ally. Every situation requires thought because you're not this, and you're not that.*

"Mrs. Bunker. I need to get you up so I can change the sheets." Ally shook the old woman's shoulder and her tiny eyes peeked through her flesh.

"Hello Ally-Allison." She sang it like a song, and it made her smile. "Ally-Allison!"

Ally took hold of Mrs. Bunker's hands and pulled her up and a wave of unwashed body odor entered the room's warm air, mixing with the stale coffee, old bagels, and sweet pungent medications. Mrs. Bunker could use a hot, long shower with fragrant soap. Ally suspected the nurse who supposedly came in twice a week to take vitals and fill her pill box was neglecting crucial duties.

"Do you mind if I open the blinds?"

"Open the blinders, but not too much."

Ally depressed the button on the controls and the hurricane blinds groaned alive. They sounded like a slow-moving train, sliding north revealing a landscape of wild grapes. Beyond that, the clear blue Atlantic Ocean. She opened the sliding glass door—an inch too much could be dangerous to Mrs. Bunker's delicate disposition—then slowly walked Mrs. Bunker to the kitchen/dining room table and prepared her coffee and bagel.

Next to the coffee machine was a tiny figure of a Black woman. Mrs. Bunker had knickknacks everywhere so it wasn't surprising that there was something offensive. It wasn't as though she possessed an entire china cabinet of busty, bobbing women with eyes that went sideways, earrings that danced erotically every time you breathed on it. *Thank goodness*, she thought, *White people finally got rid of black lawn jockeys*. Her White grandmother had had one. Ally remembered her mother searching all over the state for a Black baby doll. Ally always shoved the bobbing figure behind a shelf of old cookbooks, but it kept reappearing, as if it required a fuller recognition before disappearing forever.

"Can you turn on the TV, Ally-Allison?"

Ally turned on the TV. It sat like royalty on the kitchen counter aimed at Mrs. Bunker's favorite chair, so she could watch what she called her news show.

Then Ally turned on the TV in the living room and the one in the Granny Cave where Mrs. Bunker played games on her computer and made irresponsible purchases from scam websites. Before clicking she was supposed to request Ally's opinion but Mrs. Bunker either forgot or just ignored her son's, Fred's, rules. Thoughtful and reflective were not Mrs. Bunker's strong points, yet being reactive and filter-less gave her a certain charm: Ally never knew what would come out of the nonagenarian's mouth.

Ally stripped the bed and felt the towels (not one had been used!), gathered up the dirty laundry and filled the washer. The washing machine was probably 35—as old as Ally—and the dial was broken so you had to feel-guess where start was. Ally missed a greasy dishrag in the sink, but it was so heavy with grease and food tidbits it would have contaminated the laundry. If she tossed it out, Mrs. Bunker would doubtless inquire to its whereabouts.

"How do you think I got to be so rich, Ally-Allison?" Mrs. Bunker often said with her characteristic laugh. "I'm frugal!"

Ally never mentioned the fridge's French fries rigor mortising in take-out containers, or the spaghetti sublimating into glue. Fred wisely had not told his mother how much he was paying Ally because in Mrs. Bunker's World, you paid for things, not services. And there were lots of things in the condo: flower-patterned couches, glass cabinets bursting with china and religious statues. Things passed down from generation to generation. Fancy dishes that not one human being had ever eaten from.

She washed the rag out as best she could then return to the bedroom to vacuum. There were a dozen or so prescription medicines on the small table beside the bed, some on the floor, all in various states of repose: this lid off, this bottle on its side, this one on its head, some over to the night side, some to the day side, demarcated by a line only knowable only to its inventor. This was Mrs. Bunker's organizational method. Ally had been warned not to touch anything; Mrs. Bunker's meds were carefully calibrated by an interwoven web of doctors and a tiny mistake in her regimen could be fatal.

Ally vacuumed as much of the bedroom rug as she could, then she cleaned the bathroom. Next was the Granny Cave. She picked up all the barely legible notes on paper scraps that supposedly documented Mrs. Bunker's purchases to prove to Fred she was not irresponsible. Those went into an ornate glass bowl on an end table. She gathered coffee cups, potato chip bags, frozen food tins, and forks. When the Granny Cave was clean, she had Mrs. Bunker sit in a wide stuffed chair about six feet from a large-screen TV. Ally closed the door so as not to disturb Mrs. Bunker and continued vacuuming the living room.

At 11, Ally made lunch and that was another nice perk: Fred paid her for the half hour of eating and chatting with Mrs. Bunker. Her other job, teaching sociology courses like Communities Together or Sneaky Fascism barely paid minimum wage, although the discussions and personal interaction stimulated her mind. But she made almost three times as much at Mrs. Bunker's.

She was a couple thousand dollars short of her goal to save $15,000, then she'd return to the sleepy college town in the Finger Lakes and rent her mom's basement and have her planned baby. Ally had just entered into her second trimester.

At 11:30, Ally entered the Granny Cave with a tray of salad, bowls of split pea soup and glasses of cold water. A few feet from Mrs. Bunker she set up a small folding table and chair. Sometimes when eating lunch and watching TV, Ally felt as if she were with her own mother. There was that mutual admiration and satisfaction—-love?— that developed between only women and only over time. Ally sipped her soup: rich thick split pea soup with lots of ham, expensive soup that she ate only when she worked here. Mrs. Bunker was enough of a people-person to understand that Ally was not fond of Docx News (the Docx apparently in reference to documentary, but the program was

92

entertainment) so they always watched either Turner Classics or Documentaries USA. Today they were watching *Mississippi: 1961 to 1964.*

"Do you remember that, Mrs. Bunker?"

"I do. War on Poverty and all that."

The two of them stared at the TV, black and white photos of unpainted shacks and the Black people who inhabited them, and looks of despair on the adults' faces.

"The Bible says: The poor will always be with us. Someone has to be poor."

Ally decided not to respond to that comment.

"There was the Civil Rights Movement," Mrs. Bunker said. "JFK. Robert too, both of them shot down in the prime of their lives. They were Catholic. JFK—first Catholic president. Good Christian men." Mrs. Bunker had been a Catholic, but she'd morphed into a free-singing Christian. She believed in Jesus and the teachings of Jesus and often said: *Whatever you do to the least of my brothers, that you do unto me.* Ally thought that was a good way to approach life.

"Who else, Mrs. Bunker?" Ally said, prodding her.

"Who else what?"

"Who else was assassinated?"

"Let me think." With her trembling hand, Mrs. Bunker spooned some soup into her mouth. "There was Martin Luther. Martin Luther King, Ally-Allison!"

"Right." The churning in Ally's stomach stopped, and she could enjoy her lunch again.

"Look!" Mrs. Bunker said suddenly, her shaking finger pointing at the television screen. "There he is!"

"Who?"

"Right there!"

"Where?"

"Can't you see, Ally-Allison? You need glasses? Martin Luther King. That Black man."

"Mrs. Bunker, that's not Martin Luther King. Reverend King had a moustache. He didn't wear glasses. That man is Malcom X."

Mrs. Bunker frowned, then she said: "That's a strange name."

Ally briefly summarized the importance of Malcolm X to the Civil Rights Movement and told her about Freedom Summer, June 1964, and mentioned the murders of Chaney, Goodmen, and Schwerner, a story that Mrs. Bunker said she had never heard about. She admitted that the schools never talked about Black people, except as slaves.

"But that doesn't happen anymore," Mrs. Bunker said. "The government says everyone is equal, and Black people got all their rights in the 60s. We shop at the same grocery stores. Everyone goes to school together. And they learn together about the American Way of Life. Together."

"Learn what together?"

"You know, how the world works. Look Ally-Allison, everybody got civil rights after 1965. That's what civil rights mean. Civil—ordinary people stuff, like you and me, have rights. Rights are what's due to a person. Right to a job, right to own a house. To marry. To vote. You weren't even alive then, Ally-Allison, you know, when the Blacks got the right to vote."

"It's more complex, just because they got the right, didn't mean we could use it."

"What do you mean, we?"

"I meant Black people." This was a dance, with tricky balance. "Other people threw obstacles in the way of Black voting: there were poll taxes, transportation and accessibility problems. Intimidation, Mrs. Bunker. A lot of it still exists today, especially here in Florida." She couldn't wait to leave Florida.

"Ally-Allison, understand that there are people who will always complain, because things don't go exactly their way," Mrs. Bunker said. "I know. I was brought up in a different time, when people had to take the good with the bad. This victim mentality doesn't help. If people had religion, they'd be better off. Are you religious, Ally-Allison?"

Mrs. Bunker asked Ally this question regularly and she always gave her the same answer: "I am spiritual."

Mrs. Bunker didn't know what to make of that response, so she said: "I pray along with the Black people on TV. I donate to them. That says who I am, but I don't understand their complaints. They have all the rights that we have, and now, they seem to want this special treatment, as if something is owed to them."

Ally looked at Mrs. Bunker, the old woman's drawn face, unwashed hair, her sad eyes. It was her swollen legs that made her feel sorry for this woman and others like her. Ally had been concerned enough to spend hours talking with her doctors and explaining to Mrs. Bunker in great detail their recommendations and how to implement them. It didn't seem to make any difference.

They continued to watch *Mississippi: 1961 to 1964* and eat their lunch, Mrs. Bunker in a fog, tired out from the effort of thinking.

"I don't have a lot of time left," Mrs. Bunker suddenly said. "Soon I'll be going to that better place."

"I see," Ally said, waiting, but Mrs. Bunker did not say more.

Mrs. Bunker did not do even the minimal exercise her doctors recommended which was walking up and down the outside hallway twice a day with her walker. To exercise her body or mind seemed to demand an enormous amount of energy, and the machine of Mrs. Bunker was running out of fuel. It made Ally want to leave the condo and run along the beach as fast as she could, run miles and miles because she never wanted her mind to be old, never wanted to stop growing and producing new brain cells. She never wanted to disregard any possibility for joy and happiness; she wanted space to love and to think through problems especially now because of this life inside of her, this new beginning, already breathing and syncing to her mind.

*
**

When Ally left the condo that afternoon she snatched the Black bobbing woman, slipping her gently into her backpack, thinking this is the last time. No more hiding. If Mrs. Bunker asked her, she would tell her the Black woman was in a better place. Mrs. Bunker might think about the loss, but not for long, and in the end, she would accept it.

Photography - D Ferrara

Jean Ende
The Best Is Yet to Be

Isaac put his hand under Sarah's elbow to help her up the stairs. She was a little wobblier than usual. She'd insisted on wearing those slinky high heels which made her legs look sexy but, he knew, hurt her feet. And she'd had more to drink than she was used to. So had he.

But what the hell, Isaac thought. It was an occasion. How often does a guy get to celebrate his 45th wedding anniversary? The night had required champagne and dancing and they'd certainly done it up right.

Sarah started to undress as soon as they reached the bedroom, dropping her clothes on the floor, too eager to get to bed to pick them up. She glanced at the bra lying on top of the pile. From this angle you couldn't see the prosthetic.

When they first became intimate Sarah was self-conscious about one of her breasts being larger than the other. But Isaac said it was fine. He liked variety. He called the smaller one Jr., which he claimed stood for, just right. The other one was Sr, super right.

When she found out she needed a mastectomy to have Jr removed, Sarah considered breast reconstruction so she'd have two large breasts. Isaac said it was her decision, he just wanted her to be well. But there had been complications and by the time she was declared healthy enough for reconstruction Sarah didn't want anything more to do with hospitals. Isaac never seemed to mind.

Now, as usual, he softly kissed her scar. Then, with a little more pressure, for a little longer, he kissed the other breast. "Goodnight, Jr," Isaac said. "Good-night Sr." He started to undress.

She watched him fumble trying to quickly get out of his shirt and wondered if he wanted to make love that night. She was really tired but she wouldn't refuse him, although tomorrow would be better. We'll see how it goes, she thought.

"Here, let me do that," Sarah said. "Dress shirt buttons are pretty tiny." Even with a touch of arthritis her hands were more nimble than his.

She dropped his shirt on the floor near her discarded clothes, and ran her hands over his chest. Isaac's hair was getting thin on his head, but his chest hair was abundant, a mass of white and brown curls that hid the scar. She kissed that spot, believing her lips could feel his heart beating steadily, the artificial valve doing its job.

"I'm really ready to get into that bed," said Isaac, pulling down the covers.

"Me too," said Sarah. "It's been a long night." She reached for a favorite nightgown, the burgundy color cast a rosy glow over her neck.

Isaac wondered if she thought they would end the night by making love. He hoped she remembered that nowadays he was better at sex in the morning. Well, he didn't want to refuse her. Not tonight. We'll see how it goes, he thought.

They knew how to accommodate each other. Both slept on their left sides, his chest pressed against her back, his hand reaching across her body, cupping her breast, his long legs mirroring the curve of her legs.

"Happy anniversary, babe," said Isaac. "I love you."

"Happy anniversary, sweetheart," said Sarah. "I love you too."

They kissed. A long, deep, kiss that kindled memories, promised futures. She arched her back and moved one hand under the pillow. He moved along with her, stretched his neck, shifted one of his legs, still beside her, still touching her. Sarah gave a long, deep sigh. A few seconds later Isaac sighed, equally long, equally deep. Then they were both sound asleep.

Ruth Ann Dandrea
Snow Broke Daffodils

The spring after the winter Dad died, a late storm dumped wet, heavy snow that covered the garden for two days. When it melted, the already blooming daffodils lay alive and yellow on the dirt. Their stems ruined by the weight of the snow, unable to hold the blossoms. The ones just budded kept upright, but their greenery was blanched and they looked like the disaster survivors they were. The unbudded ones looked the way unbudded daffodils always looked, leafy spikes of green waiting, but it was clear they waited in vain. No fat bud was going to get pushed from the invisible bulb upward; no yellow-fringed trumpet of a flower was going to force its sunshine into the warming winds of April.

Spring without daffodils was such an anomaly that I started to think again about how I felt without my father in the world. As if they were somehow connected. As if Dad were calling from the mouths of the poor beautiful flowers with the wilted stems lying on the earth: I'm still here, I'm still here.

He hadn't called at all the night he died. Or if he did, my mother and I didn't hear him. We'd gone home. Despite the fact that the nursing home people had called in the evening, just before the Lawrence Welk rerun started, but conveniently after dinner was eaten and dishes were washed and wiped, to say we should come back.

We went. We stayed. We had them call a priest who came in street clothes and administered Last Rites with Dad's roommate's television blaring behind the curtain. (The curtain had been mauve when Dad was first admitted to the room, but the workers had made quick effort to change it to blue. Some things not escaping their attention.

Even if they didn't matter.) It might have been different if we'd known the priest, but as it was it didn't seem like much anything, the sacrament of the sick, but my mother and I were glad we'd had it done; Dad would've liked it, been glad for it if he'd known. If nothing else it proved an ending.

How long should we stay, my mother asked, getting fidgety in the hard-backed chair as the hour grew late.

Let's stay until we would usually go to bed, I suggested.

We should stay however long it takes, the voice in my own head chided. But I was tired, too. And uncomfortable. We sat on either side of Dad's bed holding his hot, hot hands. My mother feeling under the sheets to see if his feet and legs were cold the way my grandmother's had been, just before the end. When those unbelievably short appendages (my dad's inseam measured some eighteen inches last time I hemmed pajamas for him) burned into the palms of her hands, I think she decided he would live forever, and we went home.

Reasons why it was all right for us to leave him dying there, the old man alone, tumbled from my tired brain. She's an old woman, too, and can't be expected to sit up all night long in a chair. What if he does die? She'll be too exhausted to do the things that have to happen next. What if he doesn't? How will she get through tomorrow and tomorrow and tomorrow, creeping pettily in their paces? Could I have driven her the half hour home and driven myself back at midnight to sit and wait? Why not? Except that it would have worried her, made her feel guilty.

People often wait until their loved ones are out of the room to go to wherever we go when we die. My cousin, a hospice worker, assured me. And that might assuage if he'd died soon. But he didn't. He lived the whole night long, alone, and to tell you the truth, I'm not even sure that the time of death, some seven the next morning, is the truth or just the time the aides discovered him at the shift changed and called the house just as I was making coffee. Convenient. Easy. A nice time to deal with death, fresh from a night's sleep. With a whole day ahead of us.

No days ahead of Dad, though.

He lay dead and gone.

Next time we saw him, he was dressed for his funeral, lying in the shiny metal casket my son said reminded him of his grandfather's cars. As if he were going to drive to the netherworld. Looking just like Dad, only dead. Looking for all the world, I think, as I tramp the gardens, raking last fall's last leaves from the perennials and admiring the unscathed hyacinths blooming now, and perfect, after the small scourge of snow, like those poor, snow broke daffodils, lying yellowy on the earth. Waiting. For nothing but decay. Living out the last of lonely lives with nobody noticing.

I prop them up when I walk by.

Lift their sad heads tenderly.

Kiss them into soft, leafy beds.

Bid them formal and final goodbyes. Making sure I am there. That they know I am there. That I love them lying there just as much as I loved them lifted, strong, and full of spring song, calling out lyrics from Dean Martin, Sinatra, Frankie Laine, shouting "Mule Train," out the open car window on Sunday night rides home from my grandmother's, in a dangerous part of town, worrying my mother and risking everything to entertain me in the backseat loving it. Loving all of it so much.

Photography – B. Carroll

Nancy Matsunaga
Emergence

When the shots rang out, Eileen was ten counts under. It could have been worse: she could have given birth. She feels the tug of something live and distant, a hand shaking her shoulder like she's a small tree with dead leaves. Then, nothing.

Her eyes open. An echo is suspended in the air around her, an unanswered question. A burnt smell hits the back of her throat, the memory of smoke. She tries to remember what this place is. Her skin is cold and tingling. She lies naked beneath a paper sheet. A metallic wetness underneath her from where the speculum was. She remembers.

The room is empty, now, trembling under the fluorescents, tubes and latex discarded all around her like shed snakeskins. Medical machinery hulking in the corners, silent, menacing. A brisk rippling of recent movement in the air tells her the doctor and the nurse must have just left. She doesn't blame them for beating a rapid retreat. She would have done the same. Should have, a long time ago.

Hoarse, urgent voices ricochet off the walls. She understands she has to go. In a stupor she stands, pulls on her jeans and sweatshirt, and stumbles out, leaving the stained paper gown and sheet strewn in her wake. She's half-blind and groggy, the veil of anesthesia still enfolding her. Everything is fuzzy at the edges, just like in the dreams she always has about intruders in her house, those dreams where she's trying to scream but can't, where she keeps rubbing at her eyes as though it will make everything come clear. But nothing ever comes clear, everything stays dim, and ominous, until she manages to force herself awake. She wishes she could do that now. Her hand on the wall guides her down the hall, past the ghostly empty clinic rooms.

A nurse catches her elbow at the entrance to the waiting room. "No, hon. Don't go out there yet." Eileen clutches at the nurse's arm to keep from falling. She peers around the corner. The room flashing red, pulsating. Like a bizarre dance hall, Eileen thinks. The room beating in rhythm.

Then she sees her, on the other side of the room. Flanked by two police officers. In between them the woman looks tiny and fierce. Her straight black hair stringy and wild. Her arms pinioned behind her back, held by the officers. Her body still and taut. The woman's eyes dart around the room, land on Eileen. Eileen is frozen in place. A crazed smile pulls the corners of the woman's lips. Eileen is not sure if she is looking at her or through her, beyond her to some other reality. The officers drag the woman out. She stares at Eileen the whole way.

The waiting room is almost empty now, a scattering of black folding chairs. A few people sit, stunned, or stand in corners shifting glances from one to the other. No one speaking. Every stranger a potential time-bomb. Eileen sees Paul standing to one side. He rushes toward her, blinks with relief. A gut-punch, those eyes of his. His taut-jawed nervousness.

"Holy shit," he says. "Thank god you're all right." He reaches out to hug her, but Eileen turns away. She doesn't want him to see her pale, frightened face, or her hate. She sees a movement out of the corner of her eyes, a scuttling in the corner like a rat.

"It's done," she says. "Let's go." Paul will drive her back to their college campus. She waits for him to lead the way out, uncertain where the door is.

He steers her by the elbow. "A nurse got shot," he tells her.

"What?" Eileen asks. Her voice sounds drugged and slow. She can't make his words make sense.

"A nurse. Got shot. They medevacked her out of here."

Eileen looks back, as though she might still see the nurse, or the shooter. A sudden memory flashing in her brain like a dream half-remembered. Toward the end of the operation, Eileen woke and heard the hum of the vacuum aspirator, saw the tube protruding from under her sheet. The doctor had told her she would not remember anything. But she does remember. She remembers the vacuum aspirator, but not the gunshots, or a helicopter.

She hopes it is all finished, now.

The moon outside is cold and round, the ground iced over from a recent storm. February darkness settles its dead weight across the splayed-out land. The clinic parking lot is abandoned, an eerie silence coating everything. Eileen hears the hollow crack of a tree branch breaking under its icy load. She knows the night that she conceived. It was one week after she had ended things with Paul. He'd shown up outside her window, his face a ghostly oval, his eyes big and sorrowful. She let him in, of course. She's never been any good at saying no.

Under the parking lot lights she notices how her little Honda is rusting along the edges, rotting at its underbelly. Paul won't stop chattering, his words like drops of freezing rain pelting her face and ears. The helicopter, the police. The nurses running out from the back rooms. And before, those first terrifying moments. The shock, the not comprehending what was happening. Then the flash of realization, a split-second, the gun shot, the nurse collapsing.

"Paul," Eileen interrupts him. "Can we please just go now?"

Along the highway, beyond the strip malls and the fast food chains, are abandoned cars, the detritus of Ohio, the logical result of no inspection laws. Eileen knows that some of the cars have been sitting there for months, since the day they just stopped running and their owners left them there to die. Others are newer, possible victims of the ice storm. Their bodies hulk against the darkening sky, the only deformities in the flat vastness of the landscape.

Inside and outside the car, silence. Eileen rolls her window down a crack and leans her head back against the seat. The air coming in slices cold across her face. The roar of the wind in her ears drowning everything out. Paul doesn't look at her as he asks, "Can you close it?" Eileen doesn't respond. "Eileen, it's cold," Paul says. Eileen feels her throat tighten and her teeth clench, but she leans forward and with stiff, slow fingers rolls the window back up. She thinks again about the shooter in the clinic. How she must have planned it. The whole thing—she must have thought it out for months. How powerful she must have felt when the shot struck home. Eileen has never thought of herself as a violent person. But what she would give to feel that kind of power.

A buzzing noise starts up somewhere in the car. Paul slaps the dashboard. The buzzing grows louder.

"I saw the ultrasound," Eileen tells him. Her voice muffled, vacuumed up by the frosty air.

"You what?" says Paul. "What do you mean?"

"They have to do an ultrasound before you go in," Eileen says. "I asked to see it."

"Why would you do that?"

"I don't know. I was curious, I guess." She doesn't say, I thought I was supposed to look.

"And?"

"And nothing. It didn't look like anything. It was a tiny little white speck, this teeny speck on a pool of darkness. I could hardly see it. I'm not even sure I *did* see it." She hadn't felt anything, either. She had wanted to make herself feel something—love? guilt? rage?—but she couldn't. She hadn't felt anything now for the whole two years she had been with Paul.

"So," says Paul. "What does it have to do with anything?"

Eileen clutches the door handle tightly. A part of her wants to open the door and leap out.

"Nothing, Paul. None of this has anything to do with anything." She feels an acid taste at the back of her throat and leans forward. Her stomach clenches tight, and she claws at the window handle, grabbing it finally in both hands and rolling down the window just in time to lean her head out and vomit over the edge of the car.

"Christ," Paul says. "We need to get you back to see a doctor."

She stays leaning out the window in the cold air. Glides her hands up and down like wings. She realizes, suddenly, that she is free. She starts laughing into the icy wind.

Paul starts to pull the car over.

"Don't," she says. "I'm fine."

"You obviously aren't."

"I told my therapist that I wanted to have the baby," she laughs. "Isn't that fucking crazy?"

"It sounds pretty crazy, Eileen," Paul says. He pulls the car over to the side. "Why would you say such a thing?" He looks genuinely concerned.

Eileen laughs again. "Don't worry," she says. "I'm not sad about it. I didn't really want it. I just said that."

"Why?" he asks again, but Eileen just laughs. She doesn't know how to tell him. That it was just what she thought she was supposed to say. That her life was based on what she was supposed to say and do. That if she wanted the baby, for one fleeting moment, it was only to punish Paul. Her life was a story of punishing herself for the sake of trying to punish others.

"Drop me off at my apartment," she says. "I don't want to stay with you anymore."

The clouds break and tear apart. The moon reflects off the ice. Eileen and Paul drive the rest of the way in silence. The dividing line between the lanes beats a rhythm down the road. The buildings of their college rise before them, empty fortresses. A group of drunk students stumbles through the frigid night. Aimlessly seeking safety. Gripping on to one another and giggling as though they've never had such a wonderful time. Eileen thinks of the woman shooter, alone in her prison cell, with nothing left but an empty shell of anger. She chose her life.

And now, Eileen will choose hers.

Dark and Light - Carol Radsprecher

Jeffrey Feingold
My Left Foot

"My God, you've done it," my wife, Anna, exclaimed as she buried the heavy black handset to our home telephone in her fuzzy pink pullover so the caller wouldn't hear her.

"It's *them*!" she added.

She looked stunned.

"That's fantastic!" I blurted out. "I can't believe it! It's really them?" I paused. "Them who?"

"PBS Television," she explained, keeping the handset buried. "A producer. She wants to speak to you."

I, too, was stunned, the proverbial deer in the headlights. This was it, after all. My Big Break. My moment. Stardom was staring me in the face. The world was now my oyster. And it was about to be shucked.

I had known this day was inevitable. As surely as the sun rises each morning, as surely as the earth turns each day, as surely as you can always rely on a succulent black pastrami sandwich, with a juicy dill pickle, from Howie's Deli on Morton Avenue in Boston, I always knew that fate, however fickle, would hold fame and fortune for me.

I had known this since high school, when I felt it in my bones during the standing ovation, the thunderous applause, the electric pulse surging through my body as I bowed after mesmerizing my audience by playing an ADHD-stricken Romeo in high school. The first ever production, I suspect, of *Romeo and Juliet* in which poor Romeo had a neurological condition.

"Well hot damn, that's a new one on me," Mr. Simons, my high school drama teacher, declared. "ADHD. What the heck, Simons says, let's give it a whirl!"

It was likely the first production in which Romeo kept forgetting Juliet's name and directions to her house. It was novel. It was daring. It was undiagnosed. And it brought the house down. As fair, freckled Molly Finkleblatt—my first ever real life crush—bowed to the audience, the whistles and clapping went on for many minutes. Too many minutes. It probably would have continued for hours, had not the high school custodian asked my parents and the Finkleblatts to please stop clapping and sit down before they would be expelled.

After my glory days in high school, I put the arts behind me and went into the Navy, then college, then business. Life took over. Marriages, mortgages, middle-age. In short, grownup-type stuff. But twenty or so years later, my artistic soul was in desperate need. I turned back to acting.

I'd sent PBS my acting resume a month before, in response to their posting on an audition website. They were in search of actors for a special about Darwin. Would I play the balding, mutton-chopped, pensive Darwin, I wondered, as my wife handed me the phone? Or the terrifically handsome Alexander von Humboldt, the German naturalist and romantic philosopher who heavily influenced many of the luminaries of his generation and the next, including Darwin, Whitman, Thoreau, and Emerson?

"Jeffrey, we loved your resume," the woman on the phone said.

"Thanks so much," I burbled, "I've been waiting...Which part is it for?"

"It's for Maggie," she explained.

Maggie was my wife's Basset Hound.

"There's a scene in the show when we have a few dozen dogs, different breeds, and we'd love to have Maggie, for a Basset Hound in the mix. We're going to use the variety of breeds to demonstrate natural selection and biodiversity."

"Oh," I said, deflated.

"It pays really well," she replied. "We can use your Saint Bernard, too."

"I'll have to consult with my wife," I said. "It's her Basset Hound."

Actors include all sorts of minutiae on their resumes. Hair color, height, weight, other personal characteristics. Languages spoken. Accents. Skills. Kind of car you own. You just never know what might pique a casting agent's or producer's interest. You've got a Boston accent. Perfect. You can sing opera or rap or blues or Mongolian rock, come on in. You can blow a shofar? Ride a unicycle? Run a marathon? Play a tuba? Race sled dogs? Come in. You've got bowhunting skills, nunchuck skills, computer hacking skills, we want to see you.

Or in my case, your wife's got a Basset Hound, you're the man—or dog-for us.

"The PBS people must have seen me in *Romeo and Juliet*," I told Anna as I hung up the phone. "It would explain why they want Maggie for the show."

The next day, I told the producer that Maggie would take the role.

Maggie was a rescue dog. She'd rescued Anna.

Two years earlier, Anna was depressed, having just miscarried. Then, our dog, Andy, died. Though we still had Wenny, our big, beautiful Saint Bernard, it was too much. One morning, as I helped our daughter, Grace, get ready for school, I made a decision.

After Grace got on the school bus, I called the farm where I'd got Wenny, the puppy who'd been a surprise for Anna's birthday. I'll surprise her again. When I called, I learned they didn't have any Saint litters, but they did have a whole bunch of Basset Hound pups. Why would they breed such ridiculous looking little hound dogs when they bred magnificent, majestic Saint Bernards?

"Because," Maura, the woman who ran the farm said, "they're both wonderful family dogs."

That's all I needed. The next morning, I kept Grace out of school so she could go with me. On that chilly November day, Maura led us into the heated barn, where more than a dozen Basset pups bopped around inside a pen.

"What do you think?" I asked Grace after we watched the pups for ten minutes.

"That one," she said, pointing at a puppy who was standing on two or three others, the most energetic, crazy little whirlwind in the lot. Grace carried the pup in her lap as I drove us home.

On the way, Grace started to cry. Andy had died only a few weeks earlier, and perhaps it was too soon to get another dog. Had I made a mistake? Did we all need to grieve longer?

At home, I tip-toed into the master bedroom. "We have something for you." I opened the bedroom door and motioned for Grace to come in. She slipped the little puppy, warm and soft as velvet, under the covers next to Anna. Anna's recuperation began almost immediately; it was love at first snuggle.

Anna named the pup Maggie because the pup stole anything she could, just like a magpie. Socks, a wallet, a shiny set of keys, anything could end up under her dog bed. Even better if she could get you to chase her first in a vain effort to retrieve the stolen item. For one so low and so long, she was amazingly fleet on her stubby feet. I'd only catch her if she tripped on her ears, which she did often. They were so long, they trailed along the floor as she ran.

But what a little devil that magpie was. Of the dogs I've had over the years, Maggie was the most willful. The sweetest yet the most defiant. That defiance, somehow, was part of her charm. Maggie did what she wanted to do when she wanted to do it. I loved that about her.

On the day of the Darwin PBS shoot, Anna and I drove Maggie and Wenny to the park where their scene was to be filmed. They seemed excited to be going to their acting debut, although it may have been excitement at the chance to pee on a freshly mown field, sniff the posteriors of numerous other dogs, and enjoy a little sunshine.

Upon arrival, we were directed to a hilly green field. The director explained that he wanted all thirty or so dogs to run down the hill all together in the scene. The shot would show this crazy scramble of dozens of different dog breeds, from little, tiny pocket dogs to a goofy flat-nosed pug, to insanely long dogs, like Maggie, to huge dogs, like Wenny. And every size and shape in between, all in the same shot. Anna took Wenny up the hill on leash for the shot while I took Maggie. Upon command from the director, the owners and their leashed dogs all went barreling down the hill.

Immediately after the scene was shot, the director asked if Maggie and I could come with him for a special scene. We followed him to the top of the hill. There, he pointed down to the cameraman, who was at the bottom of the hill, a chunky heavy camera resting on top of one of his shoulders.

"OK," the director said, "in this scene, we want your Basset to look off into the distance, a little forlornly, and hold the pose, while the cameraman runs up the hill filming her. Can she do that?" the director asked. "Can you have her hold the pose while she looks a little forlornly off into the distance?"

"Are you insane?" I asked, "You've clearly never had a dog, have you? Or at least certainly not a hound dog. The good news is, she *always* looks forlorn. But the bad news is, she does what she wants, when she wants, if she feels like it."

It was true. Just six months earlier, Maggie had flunked out of school. I'd enrolled her in a training program, dropped her off in the morning, and picked her up after work. She'd be trained how to walk on leash, respond to simple commands, like sit, stay, come here, and stop chewing my expensive Italian leather wallet with the now soggy paper bills inside.

Only, when I went to pick her up one day, the trainer explained he couldn't do a thing with her.

"I've been training dogs for nigh on thirty years," he said, "but I ain't never seen no dog like this. She just won't do nothing I say, no matter what."

"What am I supposed to tell my wife?" I asked the trainer.

He screwed up his beady eyes as he scratched his scraggly brown beard, then, offered, "Why don't you tell her Maggie's comin' home. And Hell is comin' with her!"

I was disappointed. But somehow, proud, too. That's our girl, the rebel. Sticking it to the man again. Making her own rules. Wasn't that the story of my own life, too?

"So, you see," I explained to the director, as Maggie and I stood atop the hill, the gusty wind twirling her foot long ears like a pair of dancing cornstalks, "I've never been able to get her to do anything. I suppose, really, I've never been able to get any girl, canine or human, to do anything."

"Huh?" the director said, clearly puzzled. He only asked for me to make Maggie look forlornly off into the distance and to hold the pose. Not for my life story.

Later that year, Anna and I bristled with excitement the night that the PBS Darwin special was to be aired on TV. As we relaxed on our sofa, with Grace and Maggie and Wenny and popcorn—Maggie preferred kettle corn—the show began. About halfway through, the dog scene came on. To our surprise, the scene was in slow motion. As thirty plus dogs ever so slowly descended the grassy hill, there was majestic Wenny, her enormous Saint Bernard jowls slowly flapping up and down. And there, too, was Maggie, her ears taking flight in the artificially slow breeze. She looked a little like *The Flying Nun* would look if Sally Field had been a Basset Hound.

There I was, too, in my first big time, breakthrough acting role!

"Do you see it," I asked Anna?

"See what?"

"Right there, look, on screen. That's *me*. That little patch of blue—that's my sneaker. It's my left foot."

"How can you tell?" Anna asked.

"Because," I explained "did you see that hole in the toe? That's where Maggie chewed clean through. No doubt about it, it's Wenny, Maggie, and my left foot. We're famous."

A month later, a check from PBS arrived in the post. Five hundred dollars for Maggie's and Wenny's day on the set. To this day, many years later, that's still four hundred dollars more than I ever made for an acting gig. I thought about framing the check and proudly—or, perhaps, sheepishly—displaying it on our living room wall. But then I thought, no. Maggie had saved Anna's life. How would Maggie want to use the money?

The next day, after work, I hugged Anna and Grace in our kitchen. "I could use a hand with the groceries, Grace," I said.

"Sure, Dad," she replied.

I loved the look on Grace's face as she helped me carry in fifty boxes of Milk-Bone dog biscuits. That was the girls' payment, except for a small amount I reserved to buy a new pair of sneakers. I took the sneaker Maggie had chewed a hole in and hung it on the wall of our den, where it remains to this day.

Maggie passed on a few years ago, just before the start of the pandemic. I'll never take that sneaker down—a tribute to the hound who saved Anna's life, and, however fleetingly, made me a star.

Or at least, my left foot.

Image - Holly Tappen

Joel Savishinsky
The Ghost of Schubert Walks with Me in Winter

The year 2022 would have marked my parents' 81st anniversary. Their framed, World War II-era wedding picture sits atop a bookcase in my study, a few inches from photos of five people they never got to know: their great-grandchildren, the oldest of whom will soon be ready to leave for college. Looking at these faces, I have been thinking about when I myself finally left home. Diving into this memory now is only partly coincidental: between Covid and winter's cold, I have been driven both indoors and inside myself more than is usual.

In the fall of 1964, I moved out of our family's working-class Bronx apartment to go to graduate school at Cornell. That was the year I needed to study German, to figure out where the verbs go, where they begin and end, and also grasp why nouns, like columns, wore capitals. Though the university's campus was huge and enchanting, the weather soon turned gray and chilly, and most days I sought refuge in the student union's Music Room. During study breaks, I joined the people there who took turns picking out a record with a favorite composition: it was classics between classes. I would sink into a big armchair, take a deep breath and a despairing look into my German textbook. I took comfort then, as I do now, that I had grown up with the Baroque and Romantic music my mother listened to on records and a local New York radio station.

When I was younger, the irony had escaped me that—as a child of immigrants who had lost many relatives in the Holocaust—most of the composers my mother loved were German or Austrian, including Bach, Haydn, Mozart, Beethoven, and Brahms. She could never be quite

117

finished listening to Schubert's 'Unfinished' Symphony. Studying in the Music Room, I tried to draw on that soundtrack of my youth for sustenance as I faced the strange tongue before me. Being Jewish, this was not a language I was born to love, but I bore down bravely on my umlauts and gutturals by muttering my own mantra of names: Goethe, Schiller, Heine.

One afternoon, December's first upstate New York blizzard blew in: the west wind struck the Music Room's tall Gothic windows with loud waves of sleet and pebble-sized hail. Someone put on an album of *lieder*, and a tenor's mature voice, accompanied by piano and rattling panes of glass, rolled out from the speakers, commanding the room, subsuming study. I recall now that if you had listened carefully that day, you also could have heard the soft sound of books being gently closed.

At that moment, I rose from my seat and went to examine the cardboard cover of the record being played: Schubert's *Die Winterreisse*, "Winter Journey," an 1827 song cycle, settings for 24 poems written earlier by Wilhelm Müller, their titles ranging from 'Frozen Tears' and 'Flood Waters' to 'False Suns.' The liner notes explained that at age 32, this nearly-forgotten poet had passed away of a heart attack without ever hearing this vocal work performed. Schubert, the music's composer, had himself died of syphilis, aged 31, the very next year.

The short spans of the lives and creativity of these two men has now prompted both a *memento mori* and a question about my parents: what fears of loss and death had they known and lived with? I knew that earlier in their lives, when they were children—about the same age as the younger children now pictured on the shelf beside them—my parents had lived through the 1918 flu epidemic. Yet I never heard a word from them, or their parents, about that world-shattering illness. Their reticence, if that's what it was, has always mystified me. Yet it is of a piece with the silence of our culture at large, whose literature, films and arts have rarely dwelt on that traumatic, frightening global disease. It has taken Covid-19—the great-grandchild of the 1918 virus—to remind us of that time, and urge us to try to re-learn some of its lost lessons.

But how about later, during my mother and father's adulthood: what did they worry about when, in their early 30s, they had started a family of their own—roughly at the same ages that Müller and Schubert had been when they died? In the 1940s and 50s of my childhood, my parents had borne not only a son and a daughter but the weight of another pandemic that marked their time and my generation: polio. Born in 1944, I would develop mild symptoms of this terrifying disease at the age of 10; my older cousin David would be stricken with a serious case just a week before his Bar Mitzvah; and my wife would—as a four-year-old victim—end up in a special hospital ward for polio, her bed just feet away from children with iron lungs and paralyses that would end some of their lives.

Today, although I live in a country besieged by conflict and Covid-19, I still feel blessed by this anniversary's conspiracy of memory, medicine, and music. Their combined impact on me is one of hope and gratitude. For over half a century of my life, well into my own age of parenthood and grandparenting, polio has long been gone as a scourge. Having grown up in a self-proclaimed "family of worriers," I have at least been relieved of pre-occupation with that plague, which is life-enhancing in yet another way: as one global crisis ends and the next begins, it leaves me so much more time to worry about all the world's other ills. In addition, I still have the gift of music to sustain me as I move through this troubled era.

Ever since that afternoon with *Die Winterreisse* and its long-vanished storm, I have known that whatever viruses and seasons of discontent confront me, I will never have to face winter again without Schubert at my side.

Image - Holly Tappen

Natalie Harrison
Purging Diary (kept in Google docs)

August 17, frittata

August 19, tuna melt, loads of anxiety

September 7, dinner, ate late and lucas was in a bad mood. Tried puking quietly in the bathroom but he went to bed without me.

September 10, lunch with coworkers got a taco salad felt so full waited three hours before puking, was easy felt a million times better, reaffirms my belief that I can't normally eat food.

September 11, didn't eat anything all day (saw mom) beth came over had us order shake shack didn't want it threw it up after she left. Mouth tastes awful all the time no matter how many times i brush my teeth and scrape my tongue

September 21, super bad anxiety and lack of appetite/will to live reading new Sally Rooney book that's so incredible and gut wrenching and all her characters are the naturally thin types, women who forget to eat, which makes me feel jealous and hideous, Ate lunch anyway self-destructively, threw it up, almost binged but was able to go to sleep instead.

Think I threw up again later that night cant recall

Oct. 14, had lunch with lucas's folks and panicked, shoved food into my mouth, cried instantly in the car. Lucas couldn't convince me not to throw up when we got home which super rough, hardly anything came up. Want to be vegan again but I know it won't work, isn't the "solution."

October 20, didn't binge but ate too much and was scared of waking up undigested and having to throw up before work, face is so swollen i feel so sick the next day after throwing up everything is dead to me

Oct. 21, Lucas said he didnt know the act of throwing up was hard that he thought the not doing it was the hard part. He thought the hardness was purely mental. I gave him the lowdown, the fear if the food doesn't come up, how ill puke and puke until my throat swells around my fingers like a creature, so much snot and the looking at my sick gross self in the mirror between pukes, filling up a glass with metallic tap water. How does he not know this? Both he and beth say they can throw up by just thinking about it which is rude to say but also im the sick one who is jealous of this

Nov. 1, been puking every day the last week just didnt want to log it even though i promised my therapist i would. Lots of fighting and stress lucas is saying i dont love him and asking me if i want to break up which is crazy i love him so much i had nothing before him. Its like, I have an eating disorder! Beth gets how it seeps into everything. I remember binging at this party when she was in college and then going to beths apartment to throw up in her clean bathroom. I was so glad that she didnt care and kept being my friend.

Nov. 3. Had turkey sandwich but there was too much turkey, felt that panicky feeling that makes me do horribly self-destructive things

Nov. 4, felt too full after lunch, threw up at work, everyone heard me i dont even care

Nov. 24: thanksgiving leftovers

Amazingly didn't binge and purge on thanksgiving for the first time in years, was able to just have a small portion and drink wine. Lucas and i had a nice time and when we got home we shared a slice of pie and fell asleep on the couch together. I love him. I want the kind of life he wants too.

Nov. 29, tried eating breakfast total mistake threw it up refused to eat rest of the day went to bed hungry and felt at peace like I did when I used to be anorexic wish I could go back to that. How are people thin and keep food down? How am i not thin and I dont keep food down?

Dec. 1, can't even recall what I threw up but I threw up. Swore to my therapist i would stop watching what i eat in a day vlogs on youtube but i slipped up and watched five so fucking evil.

Dec. 1, veggie burger way too salty, painful purging, burst blood vessels around eyes sometimes i think im pretty when i look in the mirror after hurting myself like im for the first time really seeing myself

Dec. 23, fucking party, i had to plunge the toilet full of my vomit, remembering that time at the beach throwing up in that disgusting bathroom. Lucas asked me the other day to imagine watching myself make myself throw up and I almost cried thinking about this. Had the nightmare again where im unable to find a toilet and then have to walk over shit to get to one and then not being able to get anything out sticking all my fingers down my throat.

Dec. 25, christmas was a bad day thought about food all day but knew if i ate i wouldnt be able to hang out but ended up throwing up several times at lucas's sisters house anyway. Ate again when i got home while lucas was on his phone being cold with me which made me hate myself even more for stuffing my face in the dark. threw up again so exhausted. Wish i could flip a switch. Dont even know why hes with me. When we first got together i wasnt eating a single meal just a pretend dinner and i was spitting out food after chewing it. Everybody wants him with somebody who is well. He's so fucking wholesome.

Jan. 24, fucking party

Feb. 7, birthday dinner for beth i know she didnt expect to me eat but i was starving, wasnt able to just drink like usual its getting too hard denying myself despite that eating in public leads to binging. I think its funny that people celebrate by eating.

Feb 11, didnt throw up but had to leave work to make it through, lucas came home early and rubbed me to sleep while i cried and he gave me the millionth pep talk. Woke up fine and was glad i made it through. I used to think that emptiness made me happy but its impossible to remain empty and im not really happy just temporarily euphoric. In Rooney's Beautiful World Where Are You? theres this part where alice tells felix that when hes inside of her she feels full, i love that, i feel that with lucas. I know that at the end of the day its either him or my eating disorder.

Feb. 18: the medication is helping with my anxiety but i still fell apart during the company lunch today and in a frenzy ate a slice of pizza and then another and then a cupcake. For a minute i felt excited like i had conquered some giant fear but then the dreaded realization of the food sitting there in my stomach came and i left the meeting abruptly and threw up before anyone else came back to the office.

March 25: Been doing pretty well eating meals and keeping them down but went out to lunch with beth spontaneously and ended up throwing up at the restaurant and all the reasons why i throw up came flooding back. Maybe next year i wont be throwing up at all. My therapist told me that a large percentage of people never fully recover from an eating disorder and to expect to live with mine for the rest of my life but i still think full recovery is possible for me, despite that years and years have gone by. Even back when i was sixteen and had that feeding tube pumping Ensure directly into my stomach i remember expecting my life in the future to be free of food phobia. I'm doing this now, sitting here writing this log thinking about turning 35 in a couple months and picturing myself there, on my birthday, happy and without an eating disorder. I'm just eating cake and I'm fine.

Dianne Blomberg
I've Been Waiting for You

At sixty-three and widowed for a year from a contented twenty-five-year marriage, I sat in my husband's recliner fearful I couldn't leave.

Therapy helped me return to day-to-day functioning. It also cleared the fog to reveal loneliness, the kind that can cloud self-confidence and trick a person into believing in quick fixes and short cuts. In darkness, I asked for relief. Dear universe, I'd like to set my intention for a reprieve from Grief. He isn't finished with me yet. I won't stay away long. I want to find someone to distract me from this pain, from the hole in my gut. *"Be careful, Dianne."* Grief's warning.

***

"I have an Emmy." He handed me a business card with a much younger picture of himself holding what appeared to, in fact, be an Emmy award. He was a work acquaintance of a girlfriend. This was our blind date, and my first as a widow.

"He loves the theatre and he's a writer too. You guys will have those two things in common—and that's a good start," she said with the enthusiasm high school wrestling cheerleaders show during state finals. I expected pompoms. In fairness, maybe she was exhausted by my 11:00 pm depression calls.

Marty, a sixty-year-old with an unwarranted high opinion of himself, claimed to be a physical therapist, because "I've had so much PT, I actually treat friends and family now." An almost-college-graduate, "I'm just a semester shy of my BA from Park," (a community college). An actor conjuring something for an upcoming part, "I'm in line for several commercials and I might be moving to Houston for a movie role." A film director, "I'm reading this book on deep brain injuries to direct a documentary series." A voice-over artist, "With the money I got from my last injury at work I bought equipment for a home voice-over studio. Now, I have to learn how to use it." And a record producer...

The truth: he was a waiter, an experienced waiter at a fine steakhouse. It was his one true identity. Multiple repeat customers asked for his station when they reserved and far over-tipped because he was an attentive and thoughtful server. Occasionally, I'd eat at the restaurant and watch him pull chairs out for ladies as they sat, listen to what customers said and reply meaningfully, purchase a bottle of wine for special customers and have it open, on the table when they arrived. I liked watching him in this role. "*He's just playing a part, Dianne.*" Grief's voice warned.

The first time he invited me to his home for dinner, "Please bring the wine," was part of his invitation.

With paint chipping and weeds taking over the front lawn, his home fit into the neighborhood but didn't fit me. Inside, a few framed black and whites of himself were spread out liberally to cover the wall above a sofa in his small living room. Pointing to the only furniture there he said, "Sit down; I'll open our wine and let it breathe. Until then, here's a vodka tonic to sip on." It felt like I had been seated at "his station."

While waiting in the living room, I investigated the backyard on this early July evening. Sizable angry stickery weeds grew right up to the closed glass door, clawing to get inside. They peered through broken slats of vertical blinds he'd attempted to close. The pokey weeds clicked against the glass in the wind, sounding out some sort of warning. A shiver made me look away and try to push the slats together. "*This is not where you belong.*" I took another drink of my cocktail to quiet Grief's nudge.

That night I had planned my outfit, excited for the evening. I wore a black and white over-jacket with an asymmetrical hem, and black silk slacks. He wore his waiter pants, frayed at the cuff and a far too large summer Cuban guayabera shirt. "This was my dad's shirt. Me mum sent it to me after he passed a decade ago." I felt sad for him and a little guilty for judging him by his weeds.

"Tell me about these pictures. Are these all from past productions?" He introduced each one with the flair of an old Roman candle on its last fizzle. The photos included remembrances from high school plays, two productions from his single year of community college, and a prized photo of a small theatre presentation of *Cyrano de Bergerac*. They constituted his acting career. Both his past and imagined present.

"I need to get back to the stove. It's my famous spaghetti and meat sauce."

"Sure smells good in there," I called out from the worn brocade sofa.

Unannounced, I popped into the kitchen to watch him pour a bottle of Ragu into a skillet of ground beef backstroking in grease. My stomach started gurgling in disgust. I returned to judging.

At dinner I asked, "How did you win that Emmy?" It stood atop a leaning bookshelf in the dining area.

"A friend of mine worked for the local PBS in Philly and I read the copy on a thirty-second public service announcement."

"How long ago did you win this?"

"Several years back. But I have a lot of irons in the fire for upcoming voice-overs."

"I see."

"I understand you're a writer?" Since there wasn't more content to discuss around the Emmy, I changed the subject.

"I'm nearly done with a fantasy book. I've got some interest from an agent in New York."

After dinner, he read a few pages from his unfinished manuscript. "The child stood on the train platform, waiting for her ride. A ride to the mystical place she'd only read about." Something about a girl, who leaves home and travels through time and space, pairs up with a group of kids who all go on to become mystical magicians. The only thing missing was flying broomsticks. I was waiting for him to tell me he wrote it on a commuter train. I wanted him to shut up. But this was better than sitting in my husband's chair tonight.

A chill came over me. Grief made himself known. *"There's*

nothing for you here, Dianne."

After dinner I pulled a kitchen chair into the living room and sat across from him on the couch. I wanted distance.

I would return to that home, that brocade sofa two more times. I should have walked away but Grief holds sway over a person. I stayed in this man's grasp. Hiding.

What a fool—me not him.

Grief murmured, "You don't belong here."

***

Month two opened with us in bed for the first time. The session was forgettable, and I wanted to shower—somewhere else. He lifted his torso and leaning on one elbow started to sing showstoppers from *Phantom.* His voice, though untrained, was quite lovely. *"He's playing a part,"* I didn't disagree with Grief.

The room finally quiet, I watched while the shadow of dead tree limbs danced against his window and longed for my own bed. Grief ever at my side, *"Distractions should be brief, Dianne."*

By the middle of the month, he asked for money. "My tips were terrible this week. Do you mind picking up the entire dinner check tonight?" It is difficult to read signals while running away from the talons of loneliness. No intelligent person falls for this, I thought. This feels like a report on the evening news where I'd think, how could you be that naïve?

I did pick up the check and continued doing so for the rest of the month. I also bought a pair of work shoes and work pants for him. I watched Grief over in the corner, shaking his head, *"Distractions have a way of pulling us in."*

"Me mum (from day one he used a faux British accent) isn't well and I'd love to get back to Philly to see her." I should have caught this. No "mum" comes from Philly. "Could you help me out with the trip cost? And my fifteen-year-old daughter should go too. It might be the last time we see me mum alive. She's fading." After several minutes, "You can come along, too, if you want."

I wasn't ready to face what was waiting for me in the cellar of my heart yet. I picked up the trip cost for the three of us to visit mum. I could feel a tugging from the darkness. *"What are you doing?"*

Grief is expensive.

Marty's devotion to mum, a delightfully energetic little woman who probably lives to this day, was apparent. She bragged about his accomplishments repeating the stories he'd told me as if they were truth. She beamed, he beamed. I was stuck in the crossfire. Grief made little attempt to rescue me except for the reminder, *"Dianne, you don't belong here."*

What a fool—me not him.

***

Month three and after one of his gin-drinking afternoons, "Any chance you could help me out with my insurance premium this month?"

I don't belong here looped in my mind as if Grief and I were finally in harmony. My entire body started trembling. A need to flee took hold. At this instant loneliness seemed comforting.

It felt like I was standing on the ledge of a burning building and feared being sucked into its backdraft, "No. I won't give you any more money." The words poured out with force.

SLAM! He hit my countertop. A chill whorled around me. My breathing halted. I started shaking. I had the sudden urge to pee. Hiding from loneliness became dangerous.

"Why do you shun me and my daughter? It's because you've given me money and now you don't think I'm worthy of it. You think you're better than us. Is that the case? I was going to ask you to marry me. Well, not now!"

Wobbly but sure, I moved toward my front door with purpose. Opened it and confidently said, "We're finished here." He left immediately and with a theatrical flair that said, I've played this part many times.

Walking around my home, spraying Lysol everywhere he'd touched or sat, I was filled with gratitude for both the distraction and its exit. With a deep Lysol cleansing breath, I invited loneliness in.

That night I lit a small white candle on the kitchen island. "I've been waiting for you, Dianne." I recognized the voice inside myself and asked Grief to sit with me. Ready to engage, move through, finish, I started talking. The conversation came from down below my gut from where Grief had been patiently standing by.

I slept in my husband's recliner until the weekend when I bought a new chair. My chair.

"You will donate the old one, right?" I asked the deliveryman.

"Yes ma'am, for a fee."

Ruth Bonapace
Convulsion

I didn't bother rolling up my plaid uniform skirt as the school bus rounded the corner. I didn't care how many public school kids were outside, with their jeans and miniskirts. I saw a car in the driveway, another parked in front of the house. Cars I didn't recognize.

I thought, "Daddy's dead."

Hesitating before opening the front door, I exhaled when I heard the quiet conversation of cousins who'd arrived with trays of lasagna, cookies, and comfort.

For now, all was well. Tomorrow, it would begin again.

Nov. 4, 2020. Morning after Election Day. Waiting for my coffee to brew, I clicked The New York Times app. Fox News had called Arizona for Biden just before midnight, and The Associated Press followed three hours later. I curled up on the sofa and studied the electoral maps on other news apps. The Wall Street Journal. The Washington Post. CNN. ABC. NBC. All had Arizona still in play. In the hours since I'd gone to sleep, not much had changed, except Biden's popular vote lead had grown. I gazed out the window, watching the pale light grow brighter, trying to calm my anxiety.

My father was in a horrible car crash when I was 17, and each morning I'd leave for school not knowing if he'd survive the day. In class, lunch, orchestra practice, I was trailed by memories of the darkened intensive care room where Dad's face was swollen like a balloon about to pop.

From the window into the ICU, I could see a sheet encircling the edge of an oval on his chest, with a tangle of silver metal like children's braces holding up his sternum. I imagined a cave where you could look right into his heart. I wanted to see it, but at the same time I was grateful that metal strings, clamps, and tubes blocked the view. My own chest felt silent beneath my shallow breaths.

I followed the ventilator tube in his throat to the spider-like contraption to the monitor etching its red zig-zag. I counted the tubes in his ankles and even in the broken arm the doctors had not bothered to set, the arm he needed to land the keys on his accordion, because the odds were he wouldn't live to play it. I gazed at the bloated face. Was it really him? My mind told me yes, but my heart wasn't sure.

Day after day, Biden's Arizona lead diminished. Gray states were turning pink, light blue became dark blue, pink popped to red, others remained gray. Multiple times a day, I checked the apps: at work, over dinner, in the middle of the night. I wanted to look away, but I couldn't.

Every morning at school, there evolved a slightly altered routine. The Pledge of Allegiance on the loudspeakers, followed by Sister Marie Therese, the principal, leading the school in ritual prayers. The Apostles Creed. The Lord's Prayer. The Hail Mary.

"Holy Mary, Mother of God, pray for us sinners, now and at the hour of our death. Amen."

Newly followed by: "Let us hold in our prayers today, Rudy Bonapace."

I'd always feared prayers that strayed close to death. As a child, I'd refused to recite, "If I die before I wake, I pray the Lord my soul to take." Instead, I prayed that neither the Lord, nor anyone else, should seek my soul in the darkness of night.

But there was one prayer I dreaded more than the others:

"May their souls and the souls of all the faithful departed, through the mercy of God, rest in peace. Amen."

The Archangel Michael is said to be the champion of the sick. For this task, God had anointed not just any angel, but a warrior prince. Renaissance paintings show him with a sword and a shield. He was the one I needed most.

Changing classes in the marble halls, where even the mean girls gave glances of sympathy, I hugged my books tighter with fear and superstition. Had the hour come?

For four days, I studied the electoral maps at work, during meals, in the middle of the night. Was the gap widening or narrowing in Nevada, Pennsylvania, Georgia, North Carolina, and South Carolina? I had been worried about the outcome, but also by my growing compulsion.

Stepping outside of North Shore Medical Center on Long Island on a Saturday afternoon, I blinked my eyes and they watered in the spring sunshine. I waited near the parking lot while friends and relatives took turns visiting Dad, or more likely, saying their goodbyes. It was a protocol to which I had become accustomed for almost a month. But on this day, my mother's sister emerged from the hospital with my grandfather. Aunt Ida was grim, like the rest of us, but also highly agitated. She pulled me aside.

"He wanted to put a pillow over Rudy's head and smother him," she said.

Nonno Pio had grown up in Italy. He believed green mold on old bread was good for you, and he ate the pigeons he trapped on his roof in New York City. He also made wine, drank too much, and abused my grandmother. I looked at my aunt, wide-eyed and silent. I had never liked my grandfather. But until then, I hadn't despised him.

Nausea began to wake me every night. I'd fall asleep on the cold tile of the bathroom floor, the cotton bathmat for my pillow and a towel for a blanket, fearful that I wouldn't make it if I went back to bed. I began to brush my teeth obsessively. My gums had been bleeding for weeks. I wanted to make it stop, to scrub away the anxiety, the uncertainty. I wanted to heal myself.

A card arrived in the mail from one of my parents' acquaintances, someone they barely knew. She wrote that the pastor at her evangelical church had been praying for Dad, who he'd never met, and that God would soon welcome Dad to heaven.

I flew into a rage.

Nov. 7, 2020. On an unseasonably warm Saturday morning, I was in my garden, pulling dead plants from their pots, getting ready for winter, when I heard cars honking in the distance, as if in a parade. My smart phone was dinging and buzzing. CNN had called the election for Biden, followed by the other major networks. Friends were texting. The honking grew louder, closer. I clicked on the news. "To paraphrase President Ford, for tens of millions of Americans, 'our long national nightmare is over,'" said CNN anchor Jake Tapper.

When Dad finally was transferred out of ICU, his right arm was in a cast and there was a bandage on his throat. I pushed aside the doctor's warnings that he "wasn't out of the woods." I'd sit on the edge of his bed in the hospital ward, where he'd raise his eyebrows and make silly faces that made me smile. When he came home after almost two months, I welcomed the normalcy of doing homework while he watched TV, the end of prayers for the sick at school and, I thought, an end to fear.

Wednesday, Jan. 6. 1:15 pm. I pulled into Lowe's to buy new storage containers for my Christmas decorations. I'd been listening to the news. Pence was expected to certify the election, while Trump and his followers were rallying nearby. CNN. MSNBC. Different channel, same outrage from the talking heads. A frenzy of nothing, I thought.

That summer, I accepted a waitressing job at a family resort that my parents would take us to each year, excited at the prospect of long days in the Catskill Mountains of upstate New York. Shopping with Mom for sturdy white work shoes and uniforms—white for breakfast, pastels for lunch and black for dinner—I imagined myself following streams along woodland paths between shifts, and sprawling out on the wide lawn at night, gazing at galaxies no longer hidden by city lights.

Dad was not yet back to work, and when my family told me they were coming to the mountains for a week, I was ecstatic. I remembered how my dad loved to joke with the waitresses, and I was expecting compliments for balancing three plates on my arm. I'd learned before they'd arrived not to tip a plate down with spaghetti and to be extra careful with fried foods that could fly like frisbees if whisked from a tray too quickly. The owners assigned their table to me, and I looked forward to making Dad proud. The knot in my stomach was long gone.

Jan. 6. 1:50 pm. I got back into the car, started the ignition. Out of habit, I turned on the radio. I heard screams, sirens, and frenzied reports of rioters attacking the Capitol. I grabbed my phone and sat in the parking lot, staring at the live footage. Doors hacked open, windows smashed, people surging into the building.

But soon after my family's arrival at the resort, I was stunned to find that my genial father, who used to embarrass me by calling me Ruthie Sweetheart in front of my friends, had morphed into my harshest critic, complaining bitterly if food arrived late or a fork was missing. Dad, once a master of physical comedy who'd break into Jackie Gleason impersonations while dancing the Lindy with Mom and would have vacationers howling with his Charlie Chaplin imitations on the diving board, now spent hours inside at the resort's dark bar with a highball and a scowl.

It is well documented that patients who've had open heart surgery suffer a high incidence of post-operative depression, even though they are usually able to walk within hours and the hospital stay is short. My father didn't have heart surgery. His chest was opened because it had been shattered.

Friday, January 8. President Trump tweeted that he will not attend Biden's inauguration, shortly before he is banned from Twitter to avoid "the risk of further incitement of violence." The next day, Capitol Police Officer Brian Sicknick, assaulted by rioters, suffered two strokes and died.

I feared the Dad I'd known had died with the oncoming headlights. When he picked me up for the drive home from the Catskills, he swerved on the highway to avoid the bloody carcass of a dead dog. I began to sob and shake.

Wednesday January 20. Joe Biden is sworn in as the 46th President. I did not care about the color of Jill Biden's coat, the size of the crowd, or whose Bible had been chosen. But I was riveted by Bernie Sanders, on a simple chair in oversized mittens, like he was watching a college football game and his team was winning. Later, I copied that image and superimposed it on a photo of my front porch. A totem of hope.

Gradually, the genial father of my childhood returned, except for the scar on his throat from the tracheotomy and a misshapen wrist. Years later, after my mother had passed and his arthritis made it hard to walk, Dad looked into my eyes and said, "I couldn't live if anything happened to you."

I patted his hand and said, "Don't worry Dad, I'm not going anywhere."

I pushed away the thought: *"If I die before I wake."*

Most times, Presidential inaugurations have a reassuring sameness. In this changing of the guard, we expect a moment of good sportsmanship and civic duty, loser congratulating winner. Except for the morning of January 20, 2021, when the outgoing President was not there.

Most times, Dad came home after work, until one night, he didn't.

Image - Carol MacAllister

Tommy Vollman
Valentine Heart

It's been almost six years since you and I crowded into that tiny room at the hospital and waited. We waited and we hoped. And, eventually, our hopes grew desperate. We were there for an ultrasound; you were eleven weeks and counting. Two different technicians handled the transducer. They tipped it, turned it, slid it along and around your abdomen. The gel was warm, you joked, but the room was not, and in the hideous, low light, I stared at the grainy images that floated on the screen and tried to make sense of what I saw. You looked at the ceiling, then at me, then at the technicians. I think about what happened that day all the time.

***

One of the technicians wiped your belly and handed us off to a nurse who took us down the hall, through a corridor lined with rolling file cabinets, and showed us to a tiny room crammed with a round table and a handful of chairs. You entered first and I followed. We sat at the table, and the nurse smiled faintly.

"The doctor will be in shortly," she said. Her voice hung just a shade above a whisper. "He'll explain," she followed. Then, before either one of us could form questions, she turned and pulled the door closed behind her.

I looked at you and you stared at the table top. My heart beat against my Adam's apple, and I couldn't't swallow right. All sorts of noises clattered off the tile floor out in the long hallway and rattled underneath the thick, closed door that separated us from everything else.

139

I reached up on top of, then across the table and grabbed your hand.

Your foot tapped the carpeted floor, so reckless and seemingly unhinged. I wasn't sure if it might break or break something.

I wanted to sweep us away, to take us anywhere but the very place we were.

***

His name tag read Dr. Mich. G. Hart, but I don't remember him ever actually introducing himself. He just knocked lightly and walked in.

"Mr. Forsten?" he asked dully.

"No," I replied. "Darling. Um, Tyne." I cleared my throat. "Tyne Darling." I pointed to you. "She's Emma. Emma Forsten."

He squinted and nodded. Then, he just started talking as if we knew exactly what he was going to say, as if what he said had been scripted, then rehearsed and repeated over and over and over again.

His eyes were the absolute worst. I won't ever forget them. They barely met ours and when they did, they tore away immediately, as if we were the fire.

But we weren't the fire.

And, even though he wasn't old—probably younger than you or me—his eyes were wrapped in lines that crossed over and got tangled up in themselves. His voice slipped and slid, and you and I leaned into his words as if they threatened to push us off the edge of the Earth.

Both of us knew something was terribly wrong.

He never actually used the word miscarriage. Even there, in the hospital, no one, it seemed, dared to utter that awful, spoiled word.

"So what are you saying?" you asked, finally.

The words just kind of spilled out of your mouth. They weren't lazy or accidental, but they spilled out of your mouth like milk knocked from a glass onto a dark marble countertop. That never would have happened under normal circumstances. You hardly ever spilled anything. You were too careful, too precise.

"Are you saying that there's no baby?" you shuddered.

"What I'm saying," he sputtered, "is that there is no baby." He paused, and time slipped, moved sideways. "These things, they happen."

140

He said some other things about formation—things that I just couldn't pay attention to. Maybe you did, but I didn't.

"I—I—I—need to talk to someone else," you choked.

"You want to speak with someone else?" he replied. "They will tell you the same."

I squeezed your hand too tight.

"We just want to speak with someone else," I said. "Can you get someone else—"

"The woman—" you poked, your voice sharp and dangerous. It could've stabbed right through the walls if you would've let it. "The one we talked to last time," you added. "Dr.—"

You worked through a curtain of tears to find her name, a name that ran ragged somewhere deep in your mind.

"Dr. Wyeth," I suddenly remembered. You nodded and tears dripped from the very tip of your nose. "Is she available?" I continued. "Can you get her?"

"I'm not sure," he replied. "It's irregular." He puzzled, his face all screwed up. "You want to speak with her?" he asked.

"Yes," I said." We want to speak with Dr. Wyeth." And then, almost without pausing, I added, "We want to speak with her now."

"Well," he countered, "if you'll be patient and just let me just finish—"

I cut him off.

"No." My eyes dug into the shallows of his face. "We need to speak with Dr. Wyeth now."

"She will just tell you—"

"Please," I repeated. My voice leaked something other than exasperation. "Please. We want to speak with Dr. Wyeth." I paused. "Please."

***

Tillie.

That would have been her name. She'd have been almost six-years-old by now.

Tillie.

That should've been her name.

I'm still not sure why it isn't.

* * *

After it all happened, after you spilled what was left of her out on the bathroom floor, once, twice, then a third time, and after I cleaned it up, scrubbed the hexagonal grout lines until my callouses were gone just to be sure that there wasn't anything left, anything you'd have to see and be reminded of, we watched the Yankees. It was the 18th of September and the Blue Jays jumped out to an early three-run lead. It was nearly impossible for either one of us to care, but then the Yankees plated four in the top of the eighth inning and, like magic, erased a three-run deficit.

You fell asleep with your head in my lap, and I ran my fingers through the tangled strands of your shiny, blonde hair as you snored lightly and dreamed about things I can hardly even imagine. I cried, stifling my sobs for fear of disturbing you as Mariano gave up a ninth-inning, lead-off single to Adam Lind, followed immediately by a Colby Rasmus base hit. My eyes grew cloudy, and I could barely see Munenori Kawasaki's botched sacrifice attempt. Tears streaked my cheeks and neck and soaked the collar of my t-shirt as Rivera struck out J.P. Arencibia on three straight pitches to notch the final save of his 17-year Big League career.

I wondered, as I watched Rivera tip his cap and leave the field to a standing ovation, if anything would feel okay ever again. I wondered if anything ever had actually been okay. Maybe, I suddenly considered, that's why we told stories and watched movies, played games, wrote and read books, went to bars and got drunk and fought and fucked and fought some more. Maybe we did those things just so we could feel something, anything, other than the sense that nothing ever was or would be okay.

The TV caught my attention again and Mariano entered the frame, his hat pushed back on his head, a towel lightly draped around his neck and shoulders. At the time, no one knew it was his last save.

The interviewer, a tall, blonde woman from the YES Network, hinted at it, though.

"Mo," she said, "you're inching closer and closer."

Rivera smiled.

"You know, soon, it'll be over."

Mariano nodded and wiped his face and forehead with a corner of the towel.

"What will you do after this?" she asked. "I mean, now that such a glorious career—a surely Hall-of-Fame career—is coming to a close."

Watching Mariano, I could've sworn that his smile suddenly disappeared, but then quick as lightning, it came back.

"How will you fill that space?" the reporter smiled, "what will Mo do?"

Mariano, being Mariano, simply said something about the Yankees 'playoff hopes, then added something else about staying focused during the remaining handful of games. He left the frame, and the TV cut to a commercial break. You were asleep, your head still in my lap, and I sat there and thought about what that reporter said to Mariano. I thought about his smile and whether he hadn't answered her question on purpose.

I thought about how empty I felt, and how I couldn't really imagine what it was you were feeling. I reached for the remote and clicked off the cable box, but the TV stayed on and became a perfect rectangle of alarmingly bright blue light that stained everything: the floor, the walls, your face, my arms, everything. I shut my eyes; the rectangle still somehow visible through my closed lids. I took a few deep breaths, my eyes still closed, breaths to match yours. The blue light pushed at my eyelids and tried, it seemed, to pry them open as if it wanted to fill all of my empty spaces, the ones in my head and heart and chest. I kept my eyes closed, my breath slow and deep and still more or less in rhythm with yours. I didn't let that blue light in, didn't let it fill my empty spaces. I wanted to but to do so felt like some sort of betrayal. Still, the light pushed and it pushed. Finally, I fell asleep.

In the morning, when you woke, I asked if you were okay, and you nodded. I lied and said I was, too, and then wondered if it really was that easy.

You said you wanted to get out of the house, and so did I, so we slid on jackets and shoes, and went outside. We walked around the neighborhood, your hand tightly clasped in mine. We barely said anything at all. It was Thursday, and most everything was empty, deserted with men and women at work and kids at school. The park and the playground, the baseball diamond and the sidewalks sat idle begging to be used or maybe grateful for the break. The sun was out, and perhaps under other circumstances, it might've been beautiful. I looked at the light as it pushed through the turning tree leaves, leaves still mostly green but fading toward yellow or orange and red. I thought about how in a month or so, those leaves would fall and reveal bare branches, branches thick at first then thin and thinner still toward the ends. I thought about how much space there would be when all those leaves were gone. I thought about how much light would get through with no leaves in the way.

Kresha Richman Warnock
Jenny Moves to Albuquerque

Red Fitbit Band
Purple soft top queen-sized airbed
Pink glass cake platter
Set of six coasters—white with sand dollar etching
Cricut machine
Stainless Steel colander
Lennox fine etched crystal vase, still in box
Black plastic art material organizer
Mid-century modern table—28" by 22" (Needs Murphy's oil)
Full PURPLE six-piece comforter set
Two 16" square frosted glass tables
Three large cans of pumpkin
Two IKEA drawer organizers
Four pink glass depression era salad plates ("They were my
     mom's")
Two organic, bacon-wrapped filet mignons (frozen)
Two "thingies to make you beautiful. They didn't work for me."
     (Curling irons)

All the above are marked "gifted" on the Buy Nothing Group
Facebook page. I took the Red Fitbit band. When Jenny dropped it off,
she explained, "I've never been able to wear red. Even though I'm a
natural brunette, the color just washes me out." When she had her
colors done, that was confirmed, she says. Purple, but not purple with a
reddish tinge, is her perfect shade. I like to wear red.

She explained to me that she was moving to Albuquerque. Her landlord here in Tacoma was raising the rent too high, and she just couldn't afford it. She'd moved to Tacoma for the same reason my husband and I did a couple of years ago: rents and housing prices were more affordable in this historically working-class town than in ritzier parts of the Northwest, like Seattle and Bellevue. We had an inheritance and some savings and a pension and sold a house in Indiana, so we were able to buy a retirement condo. Jenny told me she had thought she'd be able to live comfortably, if frugally, on the $3500 income she gets with her part-time job and soon to receive Social Security. But she can't make it work.

I asked her, "Why Albuquerque? Do you have family there?" "No, it just seems like a good place to live. And housing prices are much more affordable." I tell her I've loved Albuquerque the couple of times I've visited—the high desert air, the Mexican-influenced architecture and the food. I remember visiting once and sitting out in the old town square for hours, listening to Andean pipe music on a cooling summer evening. I don't tell her I've never moved any place all by myself, where I didn't know anyone, just so I could afford to live.

She's left now. Of course, Facebook is ubiquitous, and I could reach out. She was planning to make two trips, back and forth, three eight-hour days each way, because she can't drive twelve-hour days any more. Renting a U-Haul is too expensive, and she hopes she'll be able to fit most of her clothes into the back of her hatchback, along with whatever else she was able to keep. Probably nothing red, but I hope she got to retain as many purple items as possible.

Terry Sanville
Smoke

The pigeons mating on my narrow windowsill seem amazing. I call Henry to come and see. But he's off to work without so much as a goodbye—not that I blame him. I'm sure he's glad to be free of his twisted sister, escaping to the store to bury his mind in orders and supply chain problems. They're solvable. Mine aren't.

Or that's what the doctors tell me. I always wonder: if the Elephant Man could be lovable, why can't I? But then few really love a poet. Respect? Yes. Understand? Sometimes. Love? Hard to come by. It's true that poets think on a different plane than others. Yet we suffer the same maladies, the same pains of body and spirit. "If you prick us, do we not bleed?"

I gobble the breakfast Harry left for me, push myself up from bed and hobble on swollen legs to my chair at the window for a morning snooze. A hulking garbage truck pulls into the alley in back of our building. Its metal forks stab the dumpster and raise it high into the air, as if showing off its prey to the gods, before emptying it into the truck's open maw. Motors whine, metal bangs. No one can sleep through that. The truck rumbles away and quiet returns.

I stare across the alley at the brutal architecture of the facing apartments. My spine already aches, along with the growths on my shoulders and head. The young couple on the fourth floor, second window from the right is doing it again in the kitchen. I grab my binoculars and watch their ecstasy acted out in dead silence. She can't be much older than me, beautiful, a sexual dynamo who enjoys the hell out of her boyfriend. I avoid mirrors and think about my one advantage:

my body will never change from beautiful to decrepit. I started out decrepit.

Morning TV airs *Law & Order* reruns. I watch two hours' worth, trying to find the human drama, the range of feelings that others experience, just anything really.

Keys rattle in the front door locks. "Whatcha doin', Joanne?" Cynthia calls from the entrance.

"Nothing, Cyn. Watching the same ole crap."

"You might wanna turn down the volume. I could hear it climbing the stairs."

I point to my ear. "Sorry, one more thing that's going."

Cynthia, our housekeeper and my caretaker, grins at me. "You gotta write a poem, Jo. Call it 'Same Ole Crap.' Bet you could get it published."

She hangs her sunhat on the hook near the front door and disappears into our kitchen. The refrigerator opens and closes. The pop-top of a beer can hisses in the morning heat.

"You want anything?" she calls. "I can brew a pitcher of iced tea."

"That'd be great, Cyn. And could you bring me my laptop from the dresser?"

"Sure thing, just give me a minute."

After a while Cyn enters our living room, dressed in faded jeans and a tank top. Middle-aged and divorced, she looks great to me. But she claims other gals make fun of her big butt and droopy boobs. In past times she may have been considered gorgeous. Gals don't say anything about me since I seldom go out. And when I do I wear sweatpants and a loose hoodie, sunglasses and a Covid mask. People must think I'm the Phantom of the Starbucks or maybe some disfigured gangbanger.

Cyn sets a pitcher of tea on the end table and hands me an iced glass. "Gonna be a hot one. Make sure you drink a lot."

"Yeah, give me a couple of beers and I will."

"Not good for your kidneys. You know that."

"Fuck my kidneys. I'm not gonna make it to 30 anyway. None of us do."

Cyn frowns and flops onto the sofa, ignoring my comment. "Anything special you want me to do today?"

I grin. "The couple across the alley were screwing in the kitchen again. Find me a boyfriend, will you?"

"The best I can do is turn you on to some internet sites."

"Doesn't help. Nobody in those video clips looks anything like me."

"So, I have to do some shopping this morning. You wanna come?"

"No thanks. It's already hotter than purgatory and I'd have to bundle up."

"No, you don't," Cyn says and tisks. "You don't look that bad."

"Nice try. But I know what I look like."

Cyn sits with me and watches TV then hurries off so she'll be back in time to make lunch. I finger my laptop with my good hand and start hunting and pecking fragments: sliding hands over wet slippery bodies; pigeons iridescent in the morning sun; July heat storm in Philadelphia; offering prey to the gods; this is the end, my only friend, the end.

That last fragment I recognize from my grandfather's Doors album, one of my favorites, and delete it. But I like the line's internal rhyme and play with it until a four-stanza poem emerges. I slump back into my chair, exhausted and hurting, the ice in my glass melted. I press the pitcher to my good cheek and let it chill me for a few seconds.

I check my watch. Cyn has been gone only half an hour. She'll stop at her son's house for a quick visit before hitting Giant Food. So I have at least another hour of alone time. I recline my chair, call up my favorite adults-only website and scroll through its offerings. Sweat soaks my nightgown and makes my deformities itch.

The hint of a breeze blows through the opened-a-crack window. My body shudders and it feels wonderful. But my chest tightens. It seems like an instantaneous attack of the flu. I cough a few times, the sound rattling deep in my lungs. The tightening continues and my muscles seize. I can't move or speak. The pressure now feels like a musk ox has sat on my chest and bellows into my ear. I think about the Doors song—a foreshadowing of the real thing?

My vision becomes a bright tunnel bordered in purple lightning. I try breathing but can't. Closing my eyes, I force what little air is left in my lungs outward, vacating my distorted body of the last bit of oxygen.

Suddenly, the pressure leaves me and I inhale, gasping. Opening my eyes, a cloud of grey smoke hovers in the air before me. Slowly it coalesces into a form, a genderless sad yet beautiful face with a Buddha smile.

"Your spirit is strong. Not yet."

I can't tell if I actually hear those words or if they come from inside my head. The apparition implodes and forms a thick stream of smoke that crosses the ceiling, slides over the front door and away. From down the hall a door opens and a woman cries out, then silence. The shout sounded like Mrs. Symanski in 4-B. Her husband has liver cancer and is pretty far gone. Pushing myself up, I one-hand the front door locks and step into the hallway.

Their apartment door stands open. I knock, enter and shuffle to their back room. Mrs. Symanski kneels next to the bed where her husband lies at peace. She looks up and stares at me, at the real me, sans hoodie, sunglasses, mask, or baggy clothes. Her eyes widen. She gasps and covers her mouth with a hand.

"I'm so sorry Mrs. Symanski. Do you want me to call someone?"

She nods. "Yes, please. Call . . . call . . ."

She forces herself to her feet and moves toward me. Before I realize what she's doing, she encircles my bent body with her arms and sobs onto my nightgown. Her own form, twisted with age, shakes in sorrow. I stroke her hair. I can't remember the last time I touched anyone like this. She finally releases me.

"I'm sorry," she says. "I knew this was comin', but it still . . . hurts."

"Yes, death drifts in like smoke."

She gives me a strange look then nods, sits on the bed and holds her husband's hand, a normal hand, with normal old fingers adorned with a wedding ring.

I return to our apartment and call the county coroner. Cyn has written their number in my address book next to the phone, for quick reference I suppose.

In a short while I hear a commotion down the hall, soft voices, quiet sobs, soothing words mixed with a brighter voice. Cyn pushes through the front door muscling two bulging bags of groceries.

"Did you hear what happened in 4-B?" she calls.

"Yes, I phoned the coroner for Mrs. Symanski."

"Sad, but his suffering is over. The husband always had a kind word and the wife asks about you all the time."

I listen to Cyn banging around in the kitchen, putting the groceries away, fixing our lunch while humming a slow bluesy song in her sweet contralto voice. She enters the living room carrying two trays holding monster sandwiches. We slouch on the sofa, munch our ham and Swiss on rye, and stare with glazed eyes at the TV, the sound muted. The images flash past; I doubt either of us really sees them.

"You know, we . . . we should invite . . . invite her over for tea," I murmur between mouthfuls.

"Who are you talking about?"

"Mrs. Symanski."

Cyn stares at me wide-eyed. "Really, you want to . . ."

"Yeah, why the hell not. And this afternoon, will you take me to the library?"

"Sure, Jo, sure. I'm happy you want to get the hell outta here. You know, I've been buggin' you forever to—"

"And one more thing, let's swing by the hardware store."

Cyn giggles. "What, you run out of batteries?"

"Noooo. I need to pick up a new smoke detector."

Cyn raises an eyebrow.

I'm sure she thinks I've finally lost it.

Photoraphy - B Carroll

Pam Munter
Aging Out Loud

When someone impolitely asks how old I am, it takes a minute to review the options. Most days, I feel as if I'm in my late 40s, maybe mid-50s. In reality, I'm slip-sliding towards 80. I feel good about the life I have created but how did I get to be so, well, old?

It's not as if I've wasted time. The operative motto has long been *carpe diem*. There have been multiple college degrees with careers to match, several long-term committed relationships, good friends, a wonderful son. My life has been adventurous, lived with passion at every turn, with nearly every dream fulfilled. There is no unfinished business, no bucket list.

And that's the problem. What do I do now?

There are clear advantages to being this old. Longevity and a propensity toward introspection bring a seasoned and layered perspective. Over time, a preference for complexity morphs into an appreciation for a simpler existence.

I am growing accustomed to and even amused by the sound effects of aging, if not the health complications. Some days, getting off the couch resembles a jazz trio's rhythm section. As with most in my age group, there have been troublesome health issues—breast cancer, triple bypass surgery, multiple joint replacements, TIAs, and even an alarmingly diminishing intellectual facility. "I'm Still Here," Sondheim's anthem to the aging, fits many of us. For me, what's missing is not so much youth but meaning.

Now I'm coming to the end of still another time-consuming and productive career. What's next? I can almost hear well-meaning people venturing suggestions: Volunteer! Join a social group! Travel to some exotic destination!

Earlier years of volunteering has been replaced by more distant financial contributions and, while travel remains an occasional and pleasurable pursuit, neither meet the criteria to be a central focus. I am neither depressed nor lonely. Never having been a social creature, the idea of joining any kind of group generates an involuntary shudder. Much of what success I've achieved has been borne out of a strongly independent spirit. I can be a team player if required, but I'm much better and happier as a Lone Ranger. Being alone is restorative and has been historically generative. And perhaps it will be again but at this moment, I'm in limbo.

How long do I have to figure this out? Well, we never know, do we? The family genetics portend this body to be at least a decade past its sell-by date. I have no idea what will ultimately kill me but I'm doing all I can to forestall the inevitable. There are no imminent indications of mortality and the current existential inertia and passivity run contrary to my essential nature.

This momentary pause in an otherwise meaningful life might be fertile incubation for the next era. It has been a life well-lived so far. Surely, there must be more. I know time is running out.

I remain open to possibility, but I know it's up to me. As usual.

Barry Lee Thompson
Half Life

The sky's glow is dilute, the outside air settling, and the ticks and clicks not heard in daylight have begun to emerge. Open the front door, admit the evening scents of cooling soil and stone and brick; smells of fading day, they creep across the yard and up the path to greet him like trusty old friends. A deep breath finds a note of the flowers, wild and determined, that still manage to grow in the meadows half a mile away on the farthest edge of town.

Something chases through his mind. A thing he might want to tell, to someone, anyone. Quick, grasp it before it disappears. But it goes. There is no one else here these days, just himself, and so the thought, aware of this lack of audience, scuttles away.

He's lost track of how old he is. He's tried to figure it out before, but it's been such a while since the rigmarole of cakes and cards, of happy birthdays, make a wish, three cheers. He never enjoyed the fussing, though at least it was a marker of the passing time. He was only just fifty-five at the time of the disaster, or 'incident' as it was initially called, so he could now well be sixty, say, or even maybe sixty-three or more. Who knows. Time has always been a notorious flyer, especially when you take your eyes off the clock. He might as well be a hundred and sixty for all the difference it would make. He looks down at his body. He's kept himself well, despite the challenges. The body adapts to the limits of its available resources, and his has become more defined, lean and tighter, despite his years.

What might have become of the people that lived next door? he wonders. Undergraduate students, three of them, they attended the institute on the other side of town. And there's the house further down, where the family—two women and their child, a small girl—lived. The women told him just after the birth that they only wanted the one child, one was enough, but that they'd both wished for it to have been a boy, and they felt guilty and ungrateful about that. He liked them even more for their honesty, and their containment. He hopes, even now, that he'd reassured them, that he'd let them know such thoughts were only human. He wonders if any of these people—the students, the women, the child—if any of them ever think of him, as he's thinking of them; if they wonder what's become of him, if they even care. The child might, possibly. The child, who'll probably no longer be a child at all, perhaps holds onto a diffuse memory, of a man who lived next door, in a town that was once home, a place that is no longer, that has gone, just like the era.

All the houses are empty, all along the street to the deserted highway and beyond. Nobody to bother him anymore. No comings and goings. He remembers that the day following the incident, the highway had been closed to all but departing traffic. As far as he knew, it had remained that way since. This seclusion, it's what he was after all along, perhaps, though he might have wished for its circumstances to be a little less unsafe, less extreme.

Most of the houses are unlocked. There was neither the time nor need to secure doors when leaving, and possessions remain inside, set in place. He's never bothered to investigate, other than peering through windows. In the early days, he walked about, discovering streets he'd never encountered before, marvelling at architecture and features that were new to him. He could have entered properties easily enough, and was curious at least, but the act felt intrusive even in thought, as if inhabitants might return at some point in the future. And what's the point of snooping or taking, anyway. He doesn't want more stuff, let alone other people's. Now most of the doors have become inaccessible, lost and hidden behind unkempt gardens, left to nature, though a strange nature, affected, damaged, toxic, and twisted. Thriving tendrils grasp and clutch firm to fences, and climb and march aggressively up and along walls and doors, covering all in their path. Some of the houses look from a distance as if painted a dirty dark yellow; up close as if wrapped in thick fibrous material.

He crouches down by the wild asparagus. That's what this resembles, though not in taste, not much. He picks some of the thin sprigs. The first time he saw it growing, he broke a single stalk and ate it gingerly, half expecting to feel sick or collapse. But it was tender and tasty, and he picked more, and then enough for a meal, and the more he picked the more it grew back, so now he's got this bountiful supply right in front of the house. He hasn't any care for the dangers that must lurk in the soil. He's beyond those considerations now. He's survived this far on food found in the ground.

There's a dog he sees most days, making its way down the street. A long thin animal, short fur, with a long and exceedingly whiskery snout, ears pricked high and alert. Could be wild, as he'd never noticed it before the evacuation, though it could have belonged to anyone in the town. The dog stops to sniff here and there, to look around and stare at things only it can see. It pees in three or four front yards as it goes on its way. It's clearly found a reliable source of drinking water. The dog sits and watches birds who watch back, keeps an eye out for cats. But the cats have become cleverer, hiding when they have to, and agile, more than before, and ferocious. He thinks the dog lucky to not encounter any. He's thought of tempting the dog into the house with an outstretched hand or a click of the tongue, to offer it a secure place to sleep, but the animal seems happy doing what it does.

Go inside. That's what they were told. The evacuation plan, in place for years, had been triggered and activated. Go inside, pack essentials only, and quickly, and get ready to leave immediately when called. Marshalls drove around in vans with loudspeakers, up and down every street so no one was missed. Pack your things and leave immediately. But that's not for him, packing and leaving. He'd always rather stick around, to see what happens. Both he and the dog have survived, despite the reported odds.

The news was full of it for weeks and weeks, but once the evacuation was complete, or as complete as it was going to get, the media moved on to fresher stories. And then the electricity went off suddenly one morning, shutdown or failure, and there was no way of catching any more news, and at first he worried, wondered how he'd keep abreast of developments, and then after a day or so realised that the only developments that mattered were here, right under his nose.

Many seasons have passed since then. It's become quieter and quieter as the peace has settled in even more, as the residues of previous activity die away. For a while he swore he could hear people's voices at night, the sounds of passing cars, of laughter on the streets, but the noises must have been phantoms, mere echoes of before. Now even they are gone. And the initial dust has gone, its thick layer that took days to settle all blown away. The acrid smell of chemicals is gone too, mostly, but that took a longer time, and sometimes he detects a hint when the wind's in a certain direction.

At times he gets a lurch in his chest. A familiar sensation. It dissipates at the realisation it's baseless, an anticipation of bad news he'll never receive. In all probability he'll never hear or see another person again, so there's no one to deliver news, good or bad. As the lurch departs, calm arrives, and that calm is his predominant feeling these days. Expectations of unpleasantness are his no more, though he forgets this, it's so ingrained.

He occasionally thinks that a time might come when the authorities decide to reclaim the land, that the military or police might arrive to remove him. After all, it's not as if the town has dropped off the face of the earth. It's on someone's radar. A day will come when the toxins, the radiation, have decayed sufficiently, and it's safe enough to re-enter. He's no idea what that timescale might look like, has no clue about the half-life of the substances involved, though this was discussed to death in the days after the incident, so he has a sense of its magnitude, and is confident that a time of safety is so distant that it need not trouble him, that when it comes, if ever, he'll have turned to dust, and will have blown away on the wind.

It'd be bad news if he didn't see the dog again. Or if he found the animal lying at the side of the road, succumbed to old age or contamination. But that would be his news, uncovered by him, a scoop, with no particular response expected or required. He'd be able to sit with it, the dog and the news, and assimilate it his way.

He picks a few handfuls of bushy edible weeds, and more sprigs of the asparagus-like plant, takes a gnarly lemon from the reliable tree, pops it all in his washing-up bowl then goes inside and closes the front door. He locks the door. No need, but it's a habit. Old habits die hard, they say. As always, he goes to close the curtains. Another habit. But he always pauses and then leaves them wide open so the moon will shine in, will lend the house some illumination.

He takes the bowl of wild food to the kitchen, puts it to one side by the sink, to be rinsed, to get the grit and soil off. The water supply must still be contaminated, but what he doesn't know for sure can't hurt him. He'll rinse the food later. He goes back to the living room. For now he'll just sit and watch the darkening cloudless sky, waiting for the moon to rise.

Image - Holly Tappen

Flo Golod
Prudence Loses It

Prudence flicked her wrist and shot the saltshaker straight to the bull's eye. Which happened to be the frontal sinus of her husband's forehead.

Shaped like the Eiffel Tower with a silver tip the size of a quarter inch screw bit, the weapon penetrated a small soft spot just above the bridge of Caspar's nose. The precise force honed by years of competitive dart throwing drove a hole the size of a BB into the vulnerable flesh.

As the glass tower fell to the tile floor and shattered, Caspar's blue eyes filled with tears. "Pru, why?"

"You have three other sets of Eiffel Towers. Ceramic, silver, and stainless steel."

Prudence unclenched her fingers and jabbed one towards the kitchen display that included the other Eiffel Towers, the Leaning Towers of Pisa (two identical, because one was a gift), Seattle Space Needles (plastic and ceramic), Coit Towers (one hand painted, one from a Wharf tourist trap), and Pyramids (three, two from Egypt).

Caspar fingered the swelling wound. He leaned on the fridge, staring glassily at the blood on his fingers. "Paris . . . the glass one." He pointed a shaky finger at a ceramic Eiffel. "Second Time Around. Or no, maybe Macy's. Before it closed and..." The shock of injury stalled the engine of Caspar's normally encyclopedic memory. Each of the 783 sets of salt and pepper shakers had its own origin story.

She groaned, "I'll drive you to the emergency room."

*

Pru could hear words disembodied from half-whispered sentences behind the privacy curtain. "Adult protection... domestic... social worker..."

The emergency room doctor parted the curtain, closed it deliberately, and sat down on a stool in front of Prudence. "Can you shed some light on how this happened?"

Inured to brutality and bizarre choices of weapons, he nevertheless widened his hooded brown eyes when Pru explained the source of Caspar's wound.

"Did you believe you were acting in self-defense?"

"I was defending myself against knickknacks."

The doctor leaned forward and cupped his mocha-hued hand. His impossibly clean fingers curled and uncurled, wordlessly encouraging more detail.

"He collects things. Salt and pepper shakers. But other things too."

The young doctor, Pru thought perhaps Egyptian, obviously trained to listen carefully, leaned further forward, "I don't quite understand."

"There's no place left for me. 25 years. The maps. They weren't so bad because they fold up."

The doctor nodded encouragement.

"The travel books. The worst. Fodor's, Fromm's, Rough and Lonely Planet."

"I like Lonely Planet," offered the doctor. He caught himself and rerouted. "Sorry, my bad. You're telling me he collects guide books and maps and salt and pepper shakers, and that this upsets you?"

"It unhinges me. There's no room for me or my few pathetic interests. I put a lock on my closet door when he tried to stash a box of those old spiral bound city maps."

"Hudson. Those were Hudson maps," came a surprisingly firm voice from the other side of the curtain.

"I remember those," said the doc. Pru rolled her eyes towards the heavens. Any possibly sympathetic deity was blocked by eight concrete floors above.

"They stopped publishing them in 2010," offered the patient behind the curtain. "Now King's publishes one but it's not as thorough."

"He has city maps of every city he's ever visited. Also travel books for every city, state, and country. Also salt and pepper shakers."

The doctor turned his full attention to Prudence. "I'm sure you understand that this is a form of assault, albeit a unique one. It actually is considered domestic assault."

Prudence stared at the doctor. She knew she should be feeling remorse. Or at least expressing it.

"I used to be a nice person. I volunteered for Habitat for Humanity."

"Your husband has been interviewed by our social worker, Marge Anderson. We have to file a report."

Pru's eyes widened. "I've never hit anyone, ever."

"I believe you, but I still have to report. Since this has never happened before and he wants to go home with you, I think we can take care of it today without law enforcement involvement."

Pru looked past the doctor's head at the computer monitor. The image of a police detective, picking up shards of bloodied glass off her kitchen floor, flickered on the screen briefly before she blinked it away. "I'm going to ask you to visit with Marge while we arrange the discharge. She's waiting for you in the hallway." As the doctor stood, Prudence glanced toward the curtain. "May I speak to Caspar?"

"Actually, I'm going to ask you to talk to Marge first. Then she may suggest that Caspar join the discussion before you leave."

For the first time since she'd hurtled the salt shaker, Prudence felt the force of her furious aim. A rebound. Caspar had been quiet as she drove, tight lipped, to the emergency room. He'd sighed a few times, looking out the window with the frozen peas held to his head. She hadn't expected and didn't receive recriminations. Caspar's way was passive resistance. Her way was, or had been until that day, a series of non-violent campaigns.

For two decades, Prudence had waged a cold war against accumulation—nagging, bargaining, and threats—generated nothing but minor concessions and then more accumulation. Caspar had compliantly folded his maps into well-marked banker's boxes and stacked them neatly up against the walls of what had once been their den. As the room filled, he'd moved out coffee tables and pushed the recliners close together, only inches from the television screen. One could squeeze in to watch *Downton Abbey*, but a coffee mug or glass of wine had to be balanced on one's knee.

He'd lined the basement with glass display cases for the salt and pepper shakers. At first it had been fun, a novelty that made it easy to pick out birthday presents. For years, she'd collaborated with gifts of naughty shakers, or celebrity couples, Laurel and Hardy, Sonny and Cher. As the years and collections accumulated, the cases filled. The shakers kept coming. Then in the mail, sent by well-intentioned cousins, and later, thanks to Amazon, delivered to the door in small discreet packages.

Like many childless couples, they'd arranged the small bungalow to provide a room for each person's computer and interests. Caspar filled his shelves with travel books and then began to sniff out corners that might hold another shelf or two. Eventually every wall was lined with shelves filled with travel guides and the occasional boxed set of shakers "just for fun."

When Pru first suggested that Casper rent a storage unit, he looked dismayed. "You think your maps and books will get lonely?" she snapped.

The suggestion became a demand and then a *fait accompli*. Pru rented a storage locker, handed the keys to Casper and said, "Either this stuff goes, or I do."

Caspar loaded up boxes of maps and travel books and rehomed them at Your Big Closet. While he was gone, Pru had cordoned off the empty shelves with yellow crime scene tape. When Caspar returned, looking bereft, he toured the house and looked at the empty shelves with quizzical longing.

"I want you to help me take these shelving units out. I want walls. Walls for pictures. Walls where I can practice my yoga stretches, walls with nothing, or just a decorative something or other."

Caspar bit his lip anxiously at the prospect of blank walls but he obligingly suggested moving the shelving units to the garage. Pru imagined storage for clay pots, bags of soil, and tools. Within weeks, plastic waterproof tubs of maps filled three utility shelves in the garage. Soon, three more utility shelves appeared on the back wall. Caspar found clear plastic boxes he filled with travel books. Neat labels marked them as "Midwest," "Southwest," and "Eastern Seaboard." The rest of the United States, Europe, and Mexico lurked in Storage Unit #173.

As often happened, Prudence got busy with a tight deadline and abandoned her post as wall vigilante. Caspar installed a handsome shelf with a smooth sliding cover against the recently denuded wall. "With the cover, it's like a wall and you can practice your yoga stretches against it. There's enough room at the top for some pictures or plants." Pru stalked out and retreated to the bedroom, her side still innocent of collections. She considered flight, but she was too busy. Divorce was expensive. She settled on impasse.

"Caspar, when I get done with this project, we have to get help. "

Three counseling sessions gave names and shapes to their long stand-off. Caspar recognized that his collections took over most of the house, but reminded Prudence that they were neatly kept and that initially she had enjoyed the salt and pepper shakers, and some of the books. Pru pointed out that "some" was different than 2000+ books, and that the shakers were cute until they crept up out of the basement and started encroaching on the kitchen, dining room, and sun room. Caspar promised to "greatly reduce" the intake of books and maps and to exile them to the storage unit. "But not the salt and pepper shakers. They're meant to be seen." Pru bit her tongue. With books and maps under control, two thirds of the battle would be won.

*

After the hospital and a brief visit with Marge, the beleaguered hospital social worker, and another round of mediated bickering with the marriage counselor, a truce was arranged. Less than a month later, Pru hit "send" on a report and headed to the bedroom, intending to change into gym clothes and work off deadline stress. As she wriggled into her workout pants, tighter after a week of latte and croissant-fueled technical writing, she looked up and shrieked. The best of the tower collection, glass Eiffels, ceramic hand-painted Pisas, stone pyramids, despoiled the once pristine surface of the dresser on her side of the bedroom.

Did Caspar really love his shakers more than her? Was this uncontrollable behavior or stark indifference to her needs? Was he taunting her?

The questions marched around each other as Prudence grabbed a canvas shopping bag and swept the encroachment into it, smiling the creepy grin of a mass murderer as the clinks and tinkles signaled the probability of chipped ceramic. In a homicidal trance, she hauled the shakers to the garbage and dumped them in with lethal force that assured further breakage. She stalked back into the house, grabbed her keys and left a note on the counter. "Game over, Casper. I'm outta here."

Prudence liked her apartment. Only a one-bedroom but the open floor plan meant her 750 square-foot place felt larger than the 1500 she'd shared with Caspar and his things. She abandoned the over-stuffed chairs and heavy tables for the graceful lines of mid-century modern. One book shelf and a few potted plants.

Caspar initially seemed more upset about the sacking of his collection than the decampment of Prudence. Then came the theater of divorce: the promises of reform, the begging, recriminations, and finally the tense financial negotiations. Eventually, Caspar and Prudence achieved détente. He helped her move and, a major peace offering, put together the IKEA bed frame.

Eating alone was lonely. Prudence invited Caspar over for lasagna. He arrived with red wine and a small silver box. Prudence poured the wine, then sat on her new black couch, glancing uneasily at the box on the glass coffee table. When she didn't move, Casper opened it for her, revealing two metal objects gracefully curved against each other.

"They're artist-designed salt and pepper shakers. I thought you'd like the sleek modern lines."

He paused. "I think they're kissing."

Pat Ryan
Say Hello to Pudgy
A Cautionary Tale

I don't know why I was drawn to Mrs. Birmingham. She lived alone in that brick mansion looming over Pine Hill. Her house was not typical in our town, nor was Iphigene Birmingham. She was not white-haired and soft-bosomed like my grandmother. She was hennaed and sharp-elbowed. Her eyes were two different colors—brown and green—shallow and beady. Fox fur eyes.

The first time I saw her I was eight years old, the day Sonny, my next-door best friend, and I were allowed to walk to school by ourselves. I led the way, even though I was the girl. I chose the route up Pine Hill and along High Street, past the big brick house. Every morning, I would pause at the iron gate, peek through the bars and scour every inch of the tall, stained-glass windows and pointy turrets. If Mrs. Birmingham was sitting on the porch, she would holler at us to move along. Her voice was such a raspy, barn-owl screech that I told Sonny she was a witch who flew out of her tower at night searching for little children to snatch and devour.

And yet she intrigued me. I bragged about "my witch" so much that one afternoon a small gang of kids followed Sonny and me home from school. As we neared Mrs. Birmingham's house we crept along, sticking close to the fence. When we reached the gate, I walked boldly up to it and lifted my hand to the latch. At that instant, the gate was yanked open from the other side, and there stood Mrs. Birmingham. She handed me a bag of apples. Her brown fox eye inspected the lineup of young bodies.

"There's plenty for all you sweet children," she said. "Gobble 'em up." Then she snorted and walked back through the gate.

Sonny tried to stop the gang from laughing, but they circled around me, chanting, *"Who's afraid of the big bad witch?"*

I shouted, "She *is* a witch! These apples are poisoned."

They stopped. One of the boys grabbed an apple and ate it down to the core. The kids started singing again, *"That old lady fooled you."*

I said, "She's a very rich witch. She doesn't have to cast spells every single day."

Suddenly, the gate clanged shut, and the iron latch fell into place. Like a warning shot, the sound ended all debate, and the kids scooted away. Sonny and I followed, holding hands to feign nonchalance.

......

Throughout my school years I continued to feel the pull of the brick house, and I finally entered Mrs. Birmingham's orbit for real when I was 17, and she was 75. I had taken to declining Sonny's offers of rides in his new used Chevelle, though it was an impressive color called Lagoon Aqua. I missed the old days when he would chase me around the schoolyard at recess, and I would turn on a dime and chase him back. But relations between us had become sticky. That was why I was walking alone to school one chilly February morning in my senior year.

Mrs. Birmingham must have been watching from the window as I neared her house because she opened the front door, stepped out onto the porch and beckoned me to come in. I stood uncertainly in the hallway.

She conducted a terse interview. "What is your name, young lady? What do you know? What can you do?"

I replied, "My name is Sarah, and I know a lot about the dramatic arts." Seeing her scowl, I added, "And I can type 60 words a minute."

Without further ado, she hired me to work in her library after school as a typist. Mrs. Birmingham sent an impressive number of letters every week: to lawyers, accountants, and appraisers; she ordered clothes, food, and antiques by mail. She had a cook named Bertha who lived in a carriage house adjoining the property; a cleaning woman, Millie, who came in three times a week; and Henry, a chauffeur who kept her Lincoln in a nearby garage.

She told me proudly that the three-story house was built by a prominent architect in 1887, with gables and towers in the Queen Anne style. At first, I was only allowed into the library, which I thought would be an educational place to work. But when I examined the shelves, I saw that most of the books had uncut pages.

One bookcase interested me in particular. Set in a dark corner, it was filled with leather-bound sets of English literature in alphabetical order by author—Austen and Dickens on the top shelves, Shakespeare and Thackeray on the bottom—but this bookcase was not as sturdy as the others and wobbled threateningly at a touch. The books next to the desk were on law, politics, and business, with fifty years of the "Proceedings of the Shoecrafters Association." Mr. Birmingham, I learned from his framed obituary, had been a successful businessman, active in civic affairs and "a captain in the shoe industry of New England."

After I had spent a month transcribing, typin,g and mailing Mrs. Birmingham's letters, she had Bertha lead me upstairs to the master bedroom.

In the softest voice I had ever heard, Mrs. Birmingham said, "Come in and meet Pudgy."

I walked into a surprisingly bright bedroom. The sunshine, refracted by the many cut-glass vases and mirrors, temporarily blinded me.

Holding a toy cat about eight inches long, with a polka-dotted, straw-stuffed body, she said, "Pudgy, this is Sarah."

She turned to me. "Sarah, say hello to Pudgy."

Unsure of her mood in this new environment, I reached over, said hello and patted the lumpy little head. Somehow that was the correct thing to do.

Millie, coming in with the vacuum, nodded approval. When I left that day, she stopped me at the gate and said she wanted to let me in on a secret.

"Mrs. Birmingham, being childless herself, always gives a special bonus to those young helpers who make much of her pet kitty," she said.

And so my routine shifted. Upon arrival each afternoon, I would go up to say hello to Pudgy. At the end of each week, I would total my hours and write the number in the Kitchen Accounts book. Since the expenses were listed alphabetically, "Sarah" came between "Salt" and "Sausages."

Though my salary was the same as my last year's waitressing job, the fantasy of a bonus hovered over my head. Extra money would be welcome because at that time I was applying to colleges, and I knew my parents were anxious about tuition.

My father was pleased when I asked Mrs. Birmingham for more to do besides the typing.

My grandmother, however, did not fall in line with my parents' expressions of gratitude toward Mrs. Birmingham.

Grandma cornered me in the kitchen one evening. "What's the grand dowager got you doing?" she asked.

After I gave her a description of my tasks, including the new one of helping Millie with the dusting and polishing, she said. "Tell me, my child, how does Iphigene treat you? Like the smart girl you are or like her servant, an inferior underling?"

The question confused me. I had never wondered if Mrs. Birmingham categorized me or my family as "underlings."

Grandma said, "I knew Iphigene years ago, when I worked at Ed Birmingham's shoe factory." She continued, "Iphigene *had* to live in that big house. Even after she made Ed buy it, she wasn't happy and pulled some bizarre stunts to get attention—bored, we thought, or jealous, or plain delusional."

I became defensive. Grandma had insulted my...what was she? My employer, mentor, friend, all three? Finally I said, "She's very nice, we talk about...topics: the proper clothing for girls; the correct way to pack a suitcase; how not to be cheated by tradesmen."

Grandma raised her voice. "Don't be lured by a few slippery remarks, my dear," she said. "I know a thing or two about people, and this is what I know: That cold-hearted woman on her windy hill is not like us, and she knows she's not like us, and she prefers it that way. Stay on your toes. And never, ever be ashamed of who you are."

I didn't heed Grandma's warning. I began to lavish attention on

Pudgy. I buried the desire to laugh at the pathetic misshapen thing with its foolish expression. My younger self would have made a joke with Sonny about such a silly toy. Instead, I tried to impress Mrs. Birmingham.

In May, a month before my high school graduation, a guest arrived in the brick house. And what a guest. A 20-year-old student from Paris. Her name was Délice and she was as beautiful as her name.

As I helped Bertha set up the tray for high tea, she told me all about Délice.

"Mrs. Birmingham says she's her protégé," Bertha said. "She met her three years ago at a friend's house in the south of France. Délice was a lady's maid, and Mrs. B. fell for her hook, line, and sinker," she said.

"Wow, she was a servant," I said.

"There's more," Bertha said, putting the finishing touches on the tray. "Mrs. B. is paying her tuition at that expensive French university."

"The Sorbonne?" I knew the name from typing the address.

"Yup. Full tuition and an allowance too."

Délice was friendly enough, though I had few chances to talk to her. Meanwhile, I couldn't help myself. I had stirring dreams about "a special bonus." I created scenarios in which I told my parents that my tuition would be paid in full, with an allowance.

One afternoon, while dusting the master bedroom, I heard someone in the attached sitting room, and assuming it was Mrs. Birmingham, I began to speak loudly to Pudgy about mousies and birdies. Oh, how I dishonored the bright little girl of my childhood who could defy boys and witches. In the midst of my purrs and kitty babble, Délice walked in from the sitting room and saw me holding Pudgy.

"Sarah, have you ever read Dickens?" she asked. I said no, and she laid her hand on my shoulder, leaned close to my ear and whispered, "You should." She removed her hand and stepped back, adding, "There's a copy of Great Expectations in the library, on the top shelf of one of the bookcases, the one in the dark corner. Pull the book down. Read it and compare. You might think about Miss Havisham and her penchant for 'sick fancies.'"

"Sick fancies, what do you mean?" I asked. "Are you trying to tell me that Mrs. Birmingham is crazy?" With Pudgy still in one hand, I clenched the other fist by my side and added, "Well, *you* certainly did OK by her sick fancies."

Délice flicked a fingernail at Pudgy's head. "I'm the exception," she said. "I'm the pretty protégé."

Then we heard Mrs. Birmingham's slow step on the stairs. Délice slid her silken body elegantly toward the door. "Maybe you'll finish intact," she said. "You're an innocent. *C'est possible.*"

Soon it was time for Délice to return to Paris. The day after her departure, the brick house was in a turmoil of orders and packing. "Mrs. B's going to London tomorrow," Millie said, rushing up the stairs. Henry hurried down the stairs carrying two suitcases.

With stage-fright stomach, I climbed the stairs. I entertained a flickering hope that I wouldn't be left behind.

Mrs. Birmingham was checking a list of items as Millie packed them. She turned to me and smiled. "Sarah, dear, I'm glad you arrived before I left. I would have been sorry not to say goodbye to you."

"Mrs. Birmingham, won't you want me to work for you when you return" I asked.

"Oh, heavens, no. I will be hiring a permanent assistant in London," she said. "There's no longer anything to amuse me here in this village."

"Well, goodbye, I guess," I said. "Is that all?"

A beam of sunlight flashed on her green agate eye. "There's an envelope for you in the library. A bonus for your hard work and dedication." She turned back to Millie and the packing. I was dismissed.

Each step toward the library was like a rosary bead prayed for my dream-come-true, the end that would make the means worthwhile.

The room was in the process of being emptied, the furniture covered. All that was left on the desk was a lamp and a business envelope. On it was written: *To Sarah, from Pudgy.* I ripped it open. At first I thought it was empty, for there was no card or letter inside. Then I saw the money, a $10 bill. I crumpled it in my hand. It was worse than nothing.

"It's not fair!" I hissed, tossing the money onto the floor. I started to walk away, but my knees buckled. I dropped into a wingback chair. I told myself that I had never really expected the tuition. There had never been a true bond of friendship between us. But Pudgy! Shameful visions filled my head. In a daze of self-hatred, I closed my eyes and fell asleep.

I'm eight years old. It's very cold, and I don't have a hat or coat. Snow is swirling around my head, fingering my face. Beneath the wind, I can hear children singing: "That old lady fooled you." Suddenly, Grandma and Sonny speed past me in an aqua sports car. I run after it but trip over a bag of apples and lose my Grandma.

When I woke up, it was evening and the house was quiet. I turned on the lamp, trying to remember what had happened. Automatically, I retrieved the $10 bill from the floor, and while bending down, I noticed that the bookcase in the corner was pulled out from the wall on one side. I went closer and saw that the bookcase was actually a hinged door that opened to reveal a closet.

"I looked in and gasped. In the dim light, rows of tiny eyes were staring at me from floor-to-ceiling shelves. I recoiled, then realized that they were stuffed toys — puppies, kittens, lambs, bunnies and bears — with those black-dot pupils that wiggle around behind plastic covers. Each one had a white card pinned to its head.

I went back to the desk and aimed the lamp at the shelves. How curious, I thought, every animal has a label, like in a natural history display case.

"Oh my God," I whispered in disbelief. "The last one is Pudgy." On his head was a cardboard name tag with the present date and big black letters: SILLY SARAH.

...

The next morning, I called Sonny. "Get that Lagoon Aqua Chevelle over here," I said. "I'm going to take you out for a $10 breakfast."

Photography - B. Carroll

Joel Savishinsky
The End Is Not Nigh

The end is not nigh. It is now. The world we know and tried to love has been erased and replaced...

by COVID, Trump, Putin, the internet, cellphones, hackers, populists, talking heads, empty chatter, app crap. The people who lie to themselves lie helpless under the influencers, cancellers and gender-trenders, while posting-tweeting-texting-sexting, chatting, phishing, beta-and-Spam-blocking, as well as friending-liking-linking-ghosting one another, using their VPNs to avoid getting fire-and-stonewalled so that they can message their BFFs, drink the Kool-Aid and craft cocktails, and eat pizza gummies as well as gluten-free-paleo-Keto-fasting-lo-carb regimes, choose lamely between thoughts and prayers, naked truths versus sports coverage, confessional professional athletes and memes, half-time twerking and chronic compassion fatigue syndrome, impeccable clothes and unimpeachable presidents, and harasskissing, bullypulpitting recycled politicians...

all of whom are managing to still keep company with those who, Kremlinline-and-Tuckered-outsourced, continue to truncate language by acronomizing LGBTQBIPOC and he/she/he/him/her/they and all the other identities available today under the sun and radar, even when they feel the need to apologize for apologizing and only have eyes and ears for branding, tattooing, analytics, crypto and FOMOphobia, casual sex, casual Fridays, casual and mini-serial killing, the thrill of shock and awesome, of spectacle over performance, of military euphemisms and collaterally damaged reputations, while moving with warped speed in triple-time double-speak...

though they sometimes cede the stage and front page to helicopter-snowplow parents and snowflake teenagers, kvetches like me, phone menus that have changed and beliefs that haven't, Botoxic environments, the climate change-of-the-heartsick, suffering in the dignified and Disneyfied bubble-wrapped Amazone, which features exclusive interviews with the assistant to the deputy for the special envoy to the secretary of the council of talking-heads, who whitewash, greenwash, pose, speak and link to and with NPR-PBS-NFL-BLM-WTF-OMG advice fifth columnists, proclaiming about emerging bear markets and underwater houses, while citing the views of others who are relentlessly downloading denials, dumping data and downsizing demands, but also trying not to live downstream of power plantations, lest they need to launch a SuperGoFundMeKickstarter home drive because they woke up woke today wondering if oxycodone can cure an oxymoron, or Prozac take their minds off their prostates and the red-blue-purple states, states' rights, right reason, or enable the rest of us to podcastaway our sins...

which is when we default to using the psychobabble of Babel, which—three millennia later—is still trending with the hip-hop-along talk-show word salad served with a pseudo-erotic, narcotic side of Jersey-shore-enough reality TV dinner, all blithely packed in a basket of product placements right out of the closet in your kitchen pantry, with its artisanal pâté and heirloom tomatoes, delivered and UberLyfted-Doordashed-Grubhubbed to your gated community for the family's voracious Whole Foodie diet for a small planet...

So, y'all: Eat up. You can still stream and scream and dream and cringe and twinge and binge-and-purge yourself, even though the end is no longer nigh...

It was yesterday.

Holly Tappen
Mrs. Edgewater and the Barren Orchard Trail

Canada geese don't honk thought Mrs. Edgewater, as she listened. *They emit all the vowel sounds at once, through their throat-kazoos.*

The littler birds were singing pleasantly. A sign of spring? – not yet. It was March in Minnesota. She listened until she heard the low drum of traffic behind all the trees. There went a siren, too, singing of someone's personal tragedy, be it a fire truck, a police car, or an ambulance.

Mrs. Edgewater pulled her hat over her ears, remembering her own heart attack. Ambulance. If she had another heart attack, here in the marshlands, they would find her body in the spring. Mrs. Edgewater had stepped off the paved path of The Barren Orchard Trail, preferring to field test her new garden boots by the swamp. *Bog. No. Marsh.*

She had a decision to make. Was she really willing to commit to being an artist? It took time, space, energy, resources away from other aspects of her well-crafted life. She needed to rent a studio, take classes, buy materials, meet people, and practice. Was she up for all that? The idea was exhausting. And expensive.

Even though she wore her winter coat and scarf, the air was sharp. That convoluted sky was grey. The sun god hid behind the clouds, and the pond was icy, filled with broken pearls. If the god came out, he would cast diamonds across the surface.

Mrs. Edgewater gazed around herself, isolated. What if there was a murderer hiding in the bushes, stalking her? She reached down and grabbed a river rock. It was round in her palm but knapped into a sharp edge on the other end. A weapon. They would find his body in the spring.

Everything was brown. Was there such a thing as "brown" oil paint? Could she paint these trees, grasses, cattails with their exploded hot dogs, with just one color? She looked harder. No. The grasses had yellow in that brown. The trees were thickening and had a reddish tinge to their branches. The weeping willow down next to the pond looked like a blonde with a blunt haircut. Mrs. Edgewater would have to learn how to mix a brown from the other colors, as she had read in her new art book.

Let's see.

Yellow and blue make green, but green did not apply to this landscape at all. Red and blue make purple, maybe good for shadows on the patches of snow. Yellow and red make orange. Mixed with black, that might work to paint the tall, tangled grasses. She wished she knew the difference between hay and straw. City kid. The grasses were brown. Brown had red in it. Absently, she grabbed a twig on the nearest bush. She scraped off a patch of brown bark and found, miraculously, green life inside the scratch. Quickly, she pushed the soft bark back into place. *That's what I add to a red color: green.* A million different greens and reds made up the million different brown colors down here. Mrs. Edgewater did not need a tube of brown paint at all.

She looked around intently. A flash of rust color flew by on the fat belly of a robin. *Fat? How could a bird possibly be fat after such an awful winter?*

Duh. She's pregnant, full of little blue eggs, due at Easter next month. Mrs. Edgewater wished she knew the difference between the males and female robins. She would look it up when she got home.

She stared. The mud was black under the fallen leaves. Black, like her boots. She wiggled her toes. Good. These boots fit fine for the garden. They had cost a lot.

Raindrops landed on her hat and shoulders, and the wind chilled her face. Fog swaths appeared above the pond like transparent veils. The marsh smelled rotten. Ice crunched under her feet as she made her way down to the Barren Orchard trees. They were knarly.

Old, cement grey.

Red.

There was a round dash of red hanging on the next tree. Mrs. Edgewater stood, bolted to the ground. How could that be? She then crept toward the dead tree. An *apple*? Now? Apples live in the fall. These fruit trees were supposed to be barren and lifeless after fires and floods had killed them off. That's what it said on the signs by the trail. How could this apple grow, much less survive intact after winter, and still hang from the branch?

As she approached the apple suspiciously, she saw it was elderly, wrinkled like 90-year-old skin. Desiccated. The color was maroon, and the texture was leathery and looked brittle.

"Ha!" she sang aloud to the triumphant apple. It hung at her eye level. It had not been eaten by deer, or fallen off to rot in the snow, or been ripped down by the wind. She saw there was a gash in its side. Mrs. Edgewater smiled, her face brightened and dimples appeared, for the first time in the new year. Gloves were shoved into pockets as she reached up to touch the fruit. Gently. She had no intention of being responsible for it falling from its mother.

Out of the dry gash, six seeds fell into her hand. Big, plump, brown apple seeds, as fresh as springtime. So carefully did Mrs. Edgewater bring them down to look at, the gift from the miracle apple. Making sure the apple stayed put, Mrs. Edgewater decided to plant three seeds here and three in her garden at home. She moved away from the shadows of future leaves and blossoms, uphill, away from potential flooding. Her knee sinking into the mud, she was surprised there was no permafrost here. She took the weapon rock from her pocket and scraped away the decaying leaves, exposing the rich earth. She stuck her finger in the gush and dropped in a seed. Crawling farther away, she planted the two other seeds. The three remaining seeds went into her chest pocket and the rock was stowed in her side pocket. It would come in handy in her small garden.

She stood, her knees objecting. She had not exercised in weeks. The most she could do in the wintertime was skulk around the mall in a bad mood. She felt veils of depression peel off her body. She smiled again. As she headed back to the not-so-Barren Orchard Trail, ice crackled under her boots. She looked down.

Somebody had dropped a purple candy wrapper and it was trapped under a thin glaze of ice. *Wait.*

No.

That was no candy wrapper. It was a flower, a violet. Mrs. Edgewater dropped to her knees and stared. The tiny violet was burning its way up through the clear ice to the sun and air. Its power was mighty. It conquered the ice and grew. There was another one. And another. Perfect, like lace made from a pane of glass. Beautiful, it will be, in her first painting.

She walked to her car, warm. The employees at the art supply store would not mind if she were muddy; it looked like paint.

Mandy Pennington
Save My Seat

Before more than a million people died and my jawline began regularly breaking out from wearing a mask, I went to the movies.

For some, listening to the little coughs of strangers in the dark while you're trying to pay attention to something interesting sounds like torture. It's never been easier to watch something at home, under your own blankets or in your own bed without having to pay $12 for popcorn.

But, it always felt like coming home to me.

Movies have always been a part of my life. I spent a lot of time growing up with flickers of color and light dancing off of my glasses as I watched anything and everything that seemed interesting to me at the time. Disney. Technicolor. Black and white stories where stars spoke in Transatlantic accents. *Star Wars*. *Ace Ventura: Pet Detective*. Anthony Hopkins as Hannibal Lecter. If I read the book, I would have to see the movie, even if it wasn't age appropriate. My first job at the Gateway Cinema seemed preordained: my great-grandfather was its first general manager and my mother worked there for 16 years. I can picture her pregnant belly with me inside bumping against boxes of Raisinets behind the candy stand. I filled the stand's shelves and shoveled popcorn for a little over 2 years as I started to mature into a young woman, fell in love, and started planning for my own future. It was an exciting time to watch.

When I started working at the theater, I spent just as much time seeing movies as I did working. Free admission and free popcorn is irresistible to a teenager and who was I to refuse the opportunity to see a new release before tickets even went on sale? I loved every minute my Converse shoes spent sticking to the auditorium floors. Try as you might, decades of oil and sugar add up and you'll never get them clean again. I still have dreams about working on a busy night, filling endless cups of Dr. Pepper and selling Raisinets by the case. Meditative, even.

College came and went and still, I had the movies to retreat to when my high school boyfriend broke up with me, when my stepfather died, when my family visited from out of state, and when my friends needed something to do on a warm summer weeknight. Every chance to see something felt equally like a celebration and Sunday service. Something sacred. When I didn't know what to do with myself, that's when I went. When I wanted to see that year's Oscar nominees, I went. And when I needed to purge whatever I was feeling, I went. Most of the time, I'd go alone. I found peace in being able to emote by myself in the company of strangers who couldn't see my face but who shared in my sniffs and chuckles.

My ritual was the same and I had a system: never see a movie on opening weekend—wait until the hype has died down and choose the least popular times to buy a ticket. I'd pick a Sunday morning matinee or a Thursday night showing and reserve my seat in the very last row. At the concession stand, I'd order the same thing: the kid's pack. A child-sized popcorn, a small drink, and something sweet. A little bit of everything.

The last movie I saw before the pandemic, *Little Women*, felt very much like this. I sat, that time with friends, in an empty row and let myself be taken to another place and another time for a little while. We didn't know that it was going to be the last time we'd be able to do that without worry. As I left the theater, the thought never crossed my mind that I'd be afraid to do it again.

It's hard for me to imagine feeling as at ease as I used to when I decide it's time to give it another go. I suppose that the anxiety of the past two years has changed the way I feel about what felt like a safe space. For the longest time, I haven't felt safe in my own skin, let alone in an auditorium with air and surfaces that could be dangerous—not just for me, but for those I love. I've lost that feeling of reverence for a place where I could be myself and step into the shoes of other characters at the exact same time.

When I saw *The Artist* in 2011, I wasn't expecting to be moved as much as I was. I wondered if my attention would wane without the benefit of dialogue. It had been such a long time since I'd seen a silent film. But I sat in the dark with strangers, laughing and crying my way through it, feeling absolutely overwhelmed by the beauty and simplicity. I was fully engaged—my mind, my body, and my heart. This, I thought, is what movies are supposed to be like. Or at least that's what they were like at one time and could be again. I wonder now, 11 years later, if it'll take a movie like this to get me back into a theater. Something I could fully engage in.

The first time will probably be hard. I'll buy my ticket in the very last row and scope out the seating to make sure I'm spaced as far away from others as I can be. I'll look around and remind myself that it's large and if there are only a few other people, my risk of picking up something is lower. Maybe they're all fully vaccinated and boosted and have been taking the same precautions I've been. Maybe my heart won't race when I walk in without a mask, something I still haven't gotten used to. The small crowds will be a relief but I'll probably think more about who these people are and where they've been than I ever have before. Do they feel the same way I do about being there?

Perhaps I'll be able to settle into my solitude surrounded by those who cherish the experience as much as I used to. I'd like to think they'd be more mindful of covering coughs and sneezes. Maybe everyone will pick up their own trash, too. We can share a good laugh or a cry. We can be delighted by the spectacle of it all: the performances, the costumes and makeup, the cinematography or a swirling score. We could, if we're lucky, find ourselves imagining what might happen next in a story. We can get caught up in the moment after years of languishing and flux. We'll watch something together that brings life back into focus instead of the fuzzy edges we've been living on for so long. I hope it's as good as *The Artist* in that it would remind us of what the movies could be.

And maybe, I'll feel like I can be at peace in front of a big screen again.

Photography – D Ferrara

Jill Ocone
Five South Thresholds

It's a gray day of uneasiness, not entirely unlike the gray day exactly three years ago replete with eulogies and heartache.

She dons a white gown patterned with blue and black squares comprised of small circles and triangles with rectangular ties to close the back. She rests atop a sterile, white bedsheet with a dingy blanket over her legs that doesn't match the shade of anything else in the room, except maybe the day itself.

A cold, metal chair leans against the clunky walker which rests next to a flimsy curtain that hides a sink which transforms into a toilet if she yanks the red handle suspended from the ceiling by a string.

But she's not strong enough to pull it down.

The room's walls are bare and barren, and boast no watercolor paintings of serene seascapes or soothing sunsets or anything to stimulate imagination or comfort.

She doesn't know why she's here.

A single ray of colorless light breaks through the ominous clouds and illuminates the half-full sharps bin on the wall. Her eyes track a hawk outside circling round and round five stories above, then they shift to the full dumpster five stories below teeming with discarded furniture and garbage bags haplessly thrown onto broken clocks frozen in time.

Down the hall, Martin with the gray stubble yells at the top of his lungs from behind his door, "Bear-room! I have to piss! Bear-room help!" Ten minutes earlier, he growled, "Hello, girl," from his doorway when I walked past his room wrinkling my nose from the strong odor of urine behind him. Ten minutes later, he wets his bed again and cries for his mommy.

Some families have passed by her door weeping, others have breathed sighs of relief, but she's in the middle, having endured a week of stable uncertainty and stuck in the status-quo with no clear path ahead. Discharge looms like a hurricane, but how can she be alone when she cannot remember her daughter's name, how many pills she's supposed to take with her lunch, or leaving the oven door open with the gas dialed to high?

Her breakfast of bland eggs and gummy oatmeal that she washed down with a cup of crappy decaf sits half-eaten, another meal in the cycle of flavorless monotony delivered to her door.

The incessant beep-beep-beeps echoing in the hall summon a nurse, signal high heart rates, and indicate empty fluid bags. It's that steady, monotonous, flatline tone simultaneously announcing an ending and a beginning that nobody wants to hear.

Or do they?

She's worried about her appearance, her hair, her makeup, then she remarks that the morning news woman broadcasting in front of the new museum's giant red door is beautiful.

"You should dress more like her," she insists before rolling her eyes at Martin the screamer and calling him crazy.

Anton arrives at her door with a gurney to transport her to the latest on a checklist of scans. He loads her on while wearing a smile from ear to ear, carefully covers her with a freshly washed blanket, and secures her to his cart with hard, cold buckles attached to thick, black straps.

"I'll be here when you get back," I say to her.

She turns her head to me and replies, "Thank you for caring for me. You're so nice, just like this gentleman here. What's your name again?"

Her frail hand reaches for mine, and I lean down to kiss her wrinkled skin with a tear escaping from the corner of my eye.

The nice gentleman Anton rolls her down the hall and through the threshold to where answers about what's next hopefully lurk in the dark confines of her mind.

Jennifer Bryce
The First Day

The door closes and I can hear the faint throb of the car engine as Jim sets off for work. It's just me and Annabel. I walk back down the creaking passage of our new home, alone. Play the role of a stay-at-home mum; wash the breakfast things, sweep the floor, start to make a shopping list...Is she still breathing?

I go to her room. The curtains billow. They say fresh air is good. But is she in a draught? I stand by her crib trying to assess the temperature. She's swaddled in her blanket. Can she sense my presence? Her face starts to pucker, red, almost purple—is that all right? Her little toothless, dribbling mouth—and then, the wail. I pause before the challenge of a nappy change.

I've done this countless times since we came home, but Jim was always there, within these walls. Now, this little person depends completely on me. Trembling, I lift her onto the change table. Her eyes seem to take me in. She quietens. I take a nappy from the packet. A bath? No. I think I might leave that today. Surely they don't need a bath every day? I'll give her an extra shake of powder.

There's my phone. Where is it? I can't leave her here on the change table, she might roll off. The nappy's lopsided. My hands shake. At last it's fastened. I wrap her in a confused mess. Pick her up and search for my handbag. Oh, it was Mum. I'll get back to her later. Back to the change table because the nappy is crooked, somehow. Don't panic. Start over. She is so trusting. It's as though I'm doing a good job, as though my touch is as confident as the nurses' at the hospital.

My breasts are tight, bloated. It's time for a feed. She latches on eagerly. I engulf her and we are one again, in our snuggery. Such tiny fingers, miniature ears, so perfect, and little wisps of fine blond hair. This little person has never done any wrong; she is purity, unblemished . . .

The phone again. With one hand I grapple in my bag.

'Hello?'

'Hello, dear.' My mother's voice. 'How are you getting on?'

'Just fine, thanks Mum.'

'I rang earlier, but you must have been busy.'

'Yes.'

'Done the bath?'

'Oh, yes.'

'Did she enjoy it?'

'Yes.'

'Shopping?'

'Just about to go . . .'

'Do you need a hand with anything?'

'I think everything's okay . . .'

'That's lovely dear. What are you cooking Jim for his dinner?'

'Oh—I'll decide when I'm down the street.'

'Better to have a plan.'

'Yes, Mum.'

'Well—give me a call if you need anything, dear.'

'Thanks, Mum.'

We snuggle back into the chair and I try to interest Annabel in the breast again (it's *the* breast, rather than *my* breast—all that painful instruction in hospital made it so public). She's fallen asleep. I put her back in her little crib.

They said to keep the fluids up. I make a cup of tea. I'd normally put on the news—the news? I can't believe there's another world. This is the world, it revolves around a tiny bundle in the room down the passage. My overwhelming interest is my leaking breasts. I sit in a chair and doze.

The doorbell. Heart a-patter for a moment. It's after 12 and I'm in a dressing gown with two large milk stains at the front. Haven't showered. I lie low and pray that Annabel won't cry. The doorbell sounds again. I sneak into her room. She's asleep. Footsteps on the verandah. The person has gone.

Maybe I should take a shower while she's asleep? Showering at lunch time! I keep the door open so I'll hear her if she wakens. Assuaging torrents drench my shoulders, there's so much more room here than the little cubicles at the hospital with their clammy plastic curtains that kept blowing in on me. Ah—let me stay in here forever in this little world of soothing warmth. I wash my hair. Lovely thick shampoo.

She starts to wail—then scream. No, no. I'm wet—throw on my dressing gown. Hair still dripping. 'Darling, I'm coming!' I'm cold. She's warm. We start the feed again. At last she settles; eyes shut, tiny little hand clasping my finger. Stay like this for ever, darling Annabel— innocent, rosy-cheeked, sucking.

She finishes and seems to doze. I'm hungry. I put her down. But no, she cries. She's had her rest. I thought they just ate and slept? I carry her to the kitchen and, with one hand, try to butter some stale bread. Oh – the shopping! It's 2 o'clock. I put her in the middle of our bed. I must get dressed. My hair's still wet, straggling limply around my face. She screams. 'Darling—quiet, quiet. Please don't cry!' On and on she goes. I pick her up. I cuddle her and sing, 'Hush-a-bye, lullaby, Mummy's little baby . . .' She's so worked up—red-faced. I keep singing and gradually. . . gradually . . . she calms. I daren't put her down. We sit there on the bed.

I try to put on some trousers while I hold her, but I can't do them up. Is she asleep? I move. She tenses up, legs extended—one bootie missing. So we stay there, sitting on the bed in a trance, me with trousers undone, breathing in the smell of a dirty nappy. It's not unpleasant. A surprising fact I discovered in hospital; my daughter's poo is not unpleasant. But I'll have to fix it. In fact, I should put on a load of washing.

Back to the change table. Clean her up. How awful it would be to let nappy rash invade her perfect skin. Of course, the pram—a gift from my parents; shining, resplendent with mattress and a frilly little cover. That's what I'll do. I can wheel her around with me. I tuck her in. She starts to whimper. 'No, no, little one.' I gently rock it and she settles. I wheel her to the bathroom, find a crumpled top in the ironing basket, which I put on and then I load the washing machine with one hand on the pram.

It's nearly 4 o'clock. The shopping! I imagine trying to board the bus. Too hard. Perhaps we could walk to the corner milk bar? We don't really need much. Jim won't mind take-away—again. Will she be warm enough? I daren't disturb her again to dress her in a little jacket. Instead, I throw another blanket over her, hiding the frilly cover. My purse—the keys—a bag, because I'm not sure how to attach the shopping tray to the pram. It's 20 to 5 when we set off. I almost tip her out going down the front steps—should I go backwards or forwards? Oblivious to the drama, her eyes are closed in quiet trust. We reach the gate. A familiar car pulls up.

Jim has come home early.

He gets out. Surprise flickers across his face, as he takes in my disheveled condition, my wet hair, the strewn clothing, and pram pieces. He hesitates for a moment, as if considering that this could be the new normal, then finds my face.

We both gulp. Then we smile.

Christina Reiss
The Way Out

Dean told us the only way to write authentically was to plumb our own experience. His timing could not have been worse because I was half-way through a short story about an orphan who discovers that her real parents are looking for her and, as a bonus, they are rich. I had not been in an orphanage or foster care myself. Far from it. I grew up in an intact, non-descript family in which the members played their traditional roles without complaint.

My mother was an excellent school nurse and a good enough mother. My father worked for an insurance company, calculating payouts for other people's minor scrapes or major tragedies, all with an eye toward keeping his own company profitable. I was their only child. If I wrote only about what I knew, they would be short stories indeed.

After class, I approached Dean, a hip forty-something guy in tight jeans and spiked pepper and salt hair. He affected a rebellious, burn-it-all-down attitude but he probably came from a family much like my own. I'd read some of the stuff he'd published. It didn't so much tell a story but rather offered Dean's musings about events which revolved around himself. The Dean Show. If you stripped each story down to its essential components, it would look like this:

    I.   Dean did this.

    II.   Dean thought this about what he did.

    III.   Dean considered doing this other thing.

          A.   Had Dean done so it might have turned out like this.

          B.   Because Dean didn't choose that other thing, it turned out like this.

IV.   This is how Dean felt about how things turned out.

V.   This is what Dean learned about himself.

At the end of the story, you knew a lot about Dean and very little about anything else. Of course, I knew this when I approached him but rather than start my current writing assignment over, I hoped to get a waiver from his "write what you know" edict and just go with what I had. I planned to combine false humility ("Gosh, I'm so boring and you're so interesting so what works for you will not work for me") with a bold suggestion that I was on to something new ("Doesn't an artist always reach beyond herself to an imagined world?").

I thought he might take the bait. I thought we might stay stuck on what an interesting person he was and then I could treat our conversation as permission granted. I took it as a good omen that he was alone, cleaning up the white-board, rather than ringed by clamoring college students in the usual after-class crush.

"Hey Dean," I said as casually as I could. I took pleasure in seeing him startle, a spasmodic contracting of his spinal column as if I'd jolted him with an electric cattle prod.

He turned around, his face slightly reddened, and peered at me through his wire rimmed glasses. If I had to guess, I would say he was trying to place me. I'd always suspected that he knew a lot less about the people in his classes than he pretended. For one thing, he never called us by our names. He just pointed if he saw our hands raised and was willing to let us speak. Oftentimes, he ignored the hands in the air and continued his monologue. I enjoyed watching how long my fellow students persisted, the way they slinked their hands down by their sides when it was clear that Dean would not call on them no matter how long they waited. I thought about Dean not knowing our names when he graded our work, questioning whether he could put a name to a face and wondering if it made a difference. Dean had a reputation for getting his students into the best MFA programs. He knew the right people, knew what to say. He couldn't do that for me if he didn't know my name, if I wasn't memorable in some way.

"Anna," I said, helping him out. "I was wondering if I could ask you some questions about a technique I'm trying out."

"Technique?" He raised an eyebrow. "Why don't I like the sound of that?"

"Maybe 'technique' is too grandiose," I admitted. "I am working on a story of how I wished life would turn out for someone who's suffered a harsh fate. Not me, but someone else. Kind of imagining what that would look and feel like. Unlike you, I'd have to venture pretty far outside myself to have something worthwhile to say."

As my explanation rolled out, I tried to monitor the words coming from my mouth but I couldn't quite keep up with what I was saying. I was talking too quickly, jamming it all in, shoveling it all out, as if Dean had allotted me a brief fraction of his attention and would shut me off like a spigot if I exceeded it. When I finished, I saw Dean's eyes widen, his pupils dilate as if he'd heard or seen something he liked. I figured it was the latter. I knew from experience that a man's response to a pretty, younger woman could take different routes. Some enjoyed the attention without question or analysis. Others took an instant dislike and seemed to want to humiliate the woman as if taking revenge for a slight inflicted by a pretty girl in their past. Others thought she was their due, an offering placed in a bowl at the foot of their temple. Still others seemed to believe that if the exterior was attractive, the interior was not. I didn't know Dean well enough to categorize him, so I waited until he revealed himself.

"Look, I usually get an espresso after class," he said. "It's my pick-me-up after my performance. If you want to join me, you're welcome to. I'm not going to stay here."

Dean put down the eraser and brushed his palms together, removing the debris that clung to him from class. He picked up his leather messenger bag and slung it over his back using both straps so that it looked like a child's lopsided knapsack. As he headed toward the door, he glanced over his shoulder to see if I was following him. I hadn't moved. I wanted to force him into making a more unequivocal declaration that he wanted my company.

"You coming?" he asked.

"Yes," I said.

We walked outside to the parking lot and got into his car which was nicer and dirtier than I expected. An old model BMW convertible with food wrappers on filthy floor mats. We drove several blocks and he parked in the lot behind a coffee house buzzing with activity. He took the spot reserved for the employee of the month and winked at me. When he opened the door to the coffee shop, he let it swing closed behind him. It would have shut in my face if I didn't push it open.

We sat down at one of the round café tables in the crowded room. Our server approached us, greeting Dean by name. She looked about my age with long dirty blond bangs that covered sleepy green eyes. She smiled at Dean and asked him if he wanted his usual—a double espresso with steamed milk on the side. He nodded, smiling up at her. When she turned to me, she asked if I needed a menu. The way she said it drove home I was not a regular. She also made it seem like I was too stupid to know what to order. I decided to punish her for that.

"I'll have what he's having," I said.

The woman's eyes narrowed as she glared at me. She, of course, recognized the cinematic reference. When she left our table, Dean regarded me appraisingly as if I'd scored a goal, a hockey dangle twirling behind the goalie and nipping the puck into the net.

"So, Anna," he said, "let's talk about this amazing new technique of yours that's going to set the literary world on fire."

I smiled at him, buying time. My current boyfriend called my smile radiant. He claimed I used it to distract him from what he wanted · to say, derailing our endless conversations about the status of our relationship.

"Don't you think you'll need that double espresso first?" I replied teasingly. "I think I might need one as well."

Dean smiled and let his gaze drift away, looking at the framed classic movie posters on the walls as if seeing them for the first time. We said nothing as we waited for our drinks but his eyes shifted so that they were trained on me. I kept my eyes down, my hands playing with the salt and pepper shakers and idly moving the sugar bowl. From time to time, I glanced at him and then ducked my head as if I was more innocent than my previous comments suggested. When the server set our espressos down and came back with little metal pitchers of steamed milk, Dean didn't acknowledge her. He just kept staring at me across the table.

He took a couple sips of his espresso so I took a couple sips of mine. We laughed as if this was a joke between us, two monkeys separated by a piece of glass, mimicking each other's movements.

"Okay, Anna, you've reduced me to begging. Tell me about this new technique."

"I think I may have set myself up. I hope you're not going to be disappointed. I aim to please."

I slowly poured some steamed milk into my cup and watched as an undulating swirl of cream spread out across the burnt brown surface.

"Stop holding out," Dean said. "Deliver the goods."

I felt his eyes on me but pretended to be mesmerized by what was happening inside my coffee cup. When I looked up, I told him that when I wrote I tried to take emotions I felt but was not entitled to and bestowed them on someone who was trapped in circumstances where those same feelings would be warranted. For example, I might feel alienated from my parents for no good reason. Rather than try to justify the way I felt, I created a person and a situation where those same feelings would be genuine and deserved. It seemed to work but I told him that he would be the judge of that. I looked up at him, my voice descending to a whisper, and asked him if that was all right. If that was close enough to writing about my own experience.

Dean heaved a sigh and shifted in his seat as if his clothing was suddenly too tight. He took a large sip from his espresso and then filled his cup with steamed milk, turning the mixture to a rich golden brown.

"That looks like the color of my saddle." I pointed to his cup.

"You ride?"

"I'm an excellent rider. Growing up, the only way I could communicate with my father was through sports. He was a tremendous athlete. He made the Olympic hockey team the year they cancelled the Winter Games because of the Russians. He was devastated. I don't think he ever recovered. That was going to be his ticket out."

"Out of where?"

"Out of the sameness. The small world. The crabbed existence I find myself in."

"Does your mother like sports as well?" Dean asked. He stirred his espresso with a plastic stirrer stick. He looked bored.

"No, she hates them. She's in medicine. She says her job is to fix the damage when the boys and girls leave the playground."

"I hardly think the Olympic Games constitute a playground."

I shrugged. "Well, she does."

"Sounds like your parents don't get along?" he asked, still uninterested.

"Does any couple?" I replied.

There was a long pause which neither of us tried to fill. I tried not to let it make me uncomfortable and partially succeeded. I shook my head which is something I do when I want to dislodge a thought in my mind that I don't want there. When it was gone, I smiled at Dean, turning the wattage all the way up, making sure my smile reached my eyes and set them a-twinkle.

"Well, well, well." Dean whistled through his teeth. "Who'd have guessed?"

"I hope you," I laughed. "When you grade my work, you don't offer many comments. I know just by reading your stuff that you can tell me what I need to do to improve my work. You know the editors who might publish it. You know which graduate school programs might take somebody like me. I know I have work to do. I'm willing to do whatever it takes. That's why I wanted to talk to you after class."

As I regarded him across the table, I let my eyes go wide as if I was surprised by what I was saying. I wasn't surprised at all. I only wished I'd tried it sooner. I had no idea it would be so easy. In the course of the class, Dean had mentioned his wife and young sons. He said just enough to convey the impression of one of those families in a high priced, glossy magazine ad where every family member is beautiful, aristocratic, immaculately dressed, stepping off a sailboat some place like Nantucket or the Hamptons, heading off to some exquisite meal at some exclusive private club. The kind of family where nobody spills or eats too fast or says something rude. I wasn't trying to break up his family. I had a young investment banker at home pestering me to marry him. I didn't need some older guy who taught at a second-rate college and who sold short stories to third-rate magazines.

We talked about Dean and his work as we finished our coffees. The place was emptying out so our conversation was punctuated with the sounds of metal chair legs scraping across scuffed linoleum floors. When we got up and scraped our own chair legs, Dean insisted on paying. He left the money on the table and included a meagre tip.

As we left, Dean pushed the door open, holding it as I walked throughIn the parking lot, Dean touched my forearm and said I'd given him a lot to think about. He said he would take a hard look at my work. He said he'd think about what I'd said and get back to me.

He got into his car and backed up.

He pulled out of the lot.

He didn't look back.

Sky Rooms - John Laue

Cynthia Close
The Cake Went Splat!

Pete meeting my parents is the next step. My graduation from Boston University is coming up. I am pretty damn pleased with myself, being the first in my family to go to college and to stick with it for a master's degree. So what if it was a degree in ART? Even my parents seem proud of me. They come to Boston in the spring of 1969; gram and gramps, my brother, Mom, and Dad.

What they didn't know was that they would meet my husband to be. What they also didn't know was that I had already moved in with him. Pete's divorce isn't final, but we had snagged an apartment in Eastgate, the 30-story tower in Kendall Square reserved for faculty and graduate students at M.I.T. where Pete worked as a track coach and Sports Information Director.

After the commencement ceremonies, I plan a dinner at their hotel when they would get to meet *The Man*! Pete is a relaxed, easy-going kind of guy, the kind of person everybody likes. We don't say anything to my parents about living together. I also don't mention marriage. We do talk about Pete's other family. There is some tension.

After dinner, my dad takes me aside to speak to me *privately* at the bar. This is a rare occurrence. He has had a few drinks but is not drunk. I steel myself for the onslaught. It does not come. Uncharacteristically, he is tender. "Honey, this man is trouble. You can get whoever you want. He's too old for you. Do you understand the burden of children?" We share a drink or two. I sympathize with my dad. I'm more touched by the fact that he cares enough to have this conversation with me. If he asked me if I loved Pete, I couldn't have answered.

The next day, the family goes home to New Jersey. Pete and I go home to our Cambridge apartment and wait for his divorce to become final. The papers arrive on June 1st. After divorce, Massachusetts imposed a six-month waiting period before you could remarry. Instead of waiting, the next day, we decide to drive to New Hampshire with our best friends Marge and Dave as witnesses.

The sky is a flat gray the day of the trip, mirroring my mood. I wear a very short dress with a plunging neckline in a similar shade of gray. Pete wears a suit. Marge's dress is so short it looked like a belt. She has great legs. Dave wears a vest covered with political campaign buttons. They follow us in their car.

We're in our little caravan driving north. I'm deep in thought. "Pull over." The words spill out from my unconsciousness. Pete seems flustered. Dave and Marge swerve behind us. They're confused. We all sit in silence, although it is clear that I don't want to move. Pete cajoles, jokes, nudges. Not quite begging. I am embarrassed. Something pushes me forward. We decide to drive on.

The rest is like the Beatles movie HELP! The pace is manic. We arrive at a building right over the border housing a Justice of the Peace. It's a real estate office, but they do weddings too. Pete and Marge reek of the weed they've been smoking. The geezer who is to marry us looks worried. For all he knows we are a gang of drug crazed murderers. He doesn't know whether to stare down the front of my dress or at Marge's legs. A ceramic planter in the shape of a telephone with a philodendron in it sits beside us on a desk. Dave picks it up and starts talking into it. In contrast, I'm a robot. I repeat something after the geezer reads it and then Pete says something.

It's over. We're married.

Across the four-lane highway from the office is a nondescript catering hall. We don't have reservations, but ask at the front desk if they will serve us. Dave tells the host, "this is a wedding." The host takes pity and seats us at a bare Formica table. The chef peeks out from the kitchen and laughs. We are the only ones in this cavernous space that has all the ambiance of an airport hangar. We order champagne, or as close as we can get. Food is incidental. Hysterical laughter ensues.

The waiter brings a huge, white cake decorated with roses, a gift from the hired help because no wedding should be without a cake. Our car is back in the parking lot next to the real estate office. I'm designated to carry the cake. Traffic is heavy. So is the cake. We make a dash for the car. I stumble and drop the box in the middle of the road but keep running so as not to get killed. Turning, I watch a car speeding over the box. The cake goes splat.

The motel we stay in that night is so nondescript I can't remember a thing about it. The next morning, a sense of duty compels me to call my folks. We are still in bed. I fumble with the phone on the night-table. Mom answers, "Hi, where are you?" "In a motel in New Hampshire." Silence. "Is Pete with you?" she asks. "Yes, we're married." I hear Mom suck in her breath, "You're kidding." I knew she wouldn't be happy about it, but I thought I was doing her a favor. No big wedding to plan, no expense, no debt, no dealing with in-laws she doesn't want to know. In retrospect, I see how I cheated her. Pete and I loll around, then get dressed and head back to Boston.

Pete's divorce has been brutal. He fell for a younger woman, had an affair, and didn't have a leg to stand on. He and I knew what we had done. Still, he loved his kids, wanted liberal visitation rights, and got them. Despite leaving his wife, he is a really great father. He knows how to make kids laugh and love him but can also be a disciplinarian in the best sense. After having a father who was clueless about treating children, I marry one who was a master at it.

In July 1969, we have his kids at our corner apartment on the 22nd floor. Its windows offer a glorious view of Boston across the Charles River from Cambridge. The moon is high in the sky. To the kids, we point out the shimmering reflection of that alluring orb on the river as the TV shows Neil Armstrong taking his first steps on the surface of that same moon.

Photography - Patricia Florio

William Cass
Happy Hour

With the nice weather, the restaurant had its wide doors open onto its front patio. As Louise entered through them, she smiled, taking her favorite spot at the far end of the bar. She placed her purse and light sweater on the empty stool next to her, glancing at her watch: 5:40, still enough time to make the most of happy hour if she ordered quickly. She caught the bartender's eye, holding up a credit card. A moment later, he set a glass of white wine in front of her along with a fork and knife wrapped in a napkin.

"The usual?" he asked.

She thanked him, handed him the card, and watched him tap in her order. Louise took a sip of wine and looked around her. A cool breeze carried a hint of night-blooming jasmine. The place was already bustling for so early on a Saturday and she welcomed its cocoon of soft conversation, tinkling glasses, and the easy, regular movements of others. She caught sight of herself in the mirror behind the bar, stiffened, slid a tuff of highlighted silver hair behind her ear, and took another longer sip. Even though it had been over a year since she last wore them, she still instinctively rubbed the indentation on her finger where her wedding and engagement rings had been.

A young couple maneuvered onto the stools next to hers at the bar's short end. The man sat farther away and pulled a menu so the two of them could study it together. Louise watched the man lay his free hand on the woman's thigh; she supposed they were about the same age as she and her husband, Paul, had been forty years earlier when they met.

A waiter reached around her and set a red crockery dish with three large, steaming meatballs in front of her. The meatballs huddled partially submerged in pool of marinara sauce, its aroma replacing the jasmine's. Louise unwrapped her utensils and took her first bite. She chewed slowly, closing her eyes with satisfaction. When she opened them, she found the young couple staring at her.

The woman cocked her head sheepishly and said, "Sorry. We couldn't help looking...those smell so good."

"They are," Louise said. "And on the happy hour menu, too."

They exchanged smiles. When the bartender came over, the young couple ordered the meatballs, a caprese salad, and two draft beers. Animated voices rose from a table behind Louise. She glanced at her watch, then ate more slowly than she drank. The bartender set pint glasses of beer on coasters in front of the young couple with orange slices fitted onto the rims. Louise watched them each sip away froth, then squeeze the slices as they dropped them into their glasses. Louise's eyes widened; in all the years she'd lived in Bakersfield, she'd never seen orange slices served with beer.

The woman raised her glass to Louise, the man followed suit, and the woman said, "Here's to happy hours."

Louise extended her own glass to the woman's. "Touché," she said. "And here's to May in San Diego."

They drank. Louise glanced at her watch again, caught the bartender's eye, and tipped her nearly empty glass his way. He gave her another nod. She heard the young woman ask, "Have you lived here long?"

Louise turned back and shook her head. "Only a few months. And where I come from, it's nearly ninety degrees."

"Ouch," the man said.

"So, this..." Louise waved her hand through the air. "...is lovely."

The couple continued to smile. Louise finished her last sip of wine, then asked, "Have you been to the flower show?"

"Not yet," the woman said.

"You should go," Louise told them. "I went today. Wonderful. The cut arrangements, the children's section, the arboreals, the herb garden. Just wonderful."

"So I've heard." The woman looked to the man for confirmation. "Three years and we still haven't been." He turned his gaze up towards a muted baseball game on a television above the bar. The woman leaned in towards Louise and whispered, "I'll drag him there tomorrow."

The conspiratorial gesture made something fall in Louise. She remembered often reacting similarly with others when Paul was less than responsive. The bartender replaced Louise's empty glass with a full one. Before she took a sip, she told the woman, "Don't miss the orchids. They're in a back corner of the main tent. I'd like to enter one there myself, if I'm still here next year."

"Well," the young woman said and patted her wrist, "I hope you do."

They returned to their drinks and Louise thought about her orchids. She'd brought along her two most-cherished ones in the car with her from Bakersfield, but wasn't at all sure the invitation about using her old college roommate's condo extended to the following spring. They'd only made arrangements when her old roommate offered out of the blue after posting a Facebook condolence message about Paul's passing. Louise had no idea how long her old roommate and her husband would remain away remodeling their second home down in San Miguel de Allende, though she'd made it sound as if they wouldn't be returning anytime soon.

After a few minutes, the waiter brought the young couple their food. They took turns with the small plates the way she and Paul had done so many times. She took another swallow of wine, then finished half of her second meatball and sipped more slowly at her wine as happy hour slipped well past its conclusion.

The restaurant grew busier and the early evening's light slowly descended. Without asking, the bartender brought her check, dumped her remaining meatballs into a leftover box, and took away everything but that and her glass. Eventually, the young couple mumbled goodbyes and departed. Several moments later, a voice to her left said, "This spot taken?"

Louise turned and found a tall, slender man about her age

smiling down at her and pointing at the empty stool next to the one with her purse and sweater.

"No," Louise heard herself saying. She reached for her belongings. "Here, let me..."

He placed his warm hand on hers. "No need to move your things, darlin'." He took his hand away, but his pleasant smile remained as he settled onto the empty stool. "This will do fine."

Louise smoothed her hair and stole glances at him in the mirror behind the bar as he ordered a bottle of domestic beer. Her fingertips trailed to her chest where her heart had quickened. Something in his tone reminded her fondly of old ranchers from home, but his appearance was gentler, less rough and rugged; his eyelids drooped a bit at the outside edges suggesting a quiet sort of tenderness. He wore no ring. Louise hurried the wine glass to her lips and wished it held more.

The bartender brought the man a frosted mug with the beer, but he took a healthy pull from the bottle, ignoring the mug. Louise hazarded a hasty appraisal of herself in the mirror and thought: *I've seen worse...at my age.* She thought: *Say something to him. What do you have to lose? Why do you think you bring yourself to these places, anyway, instead of microwaving yourself another dinner alone? Why'd you come to San Diego in the first place? Who are you kidding? Go on, now.*

She took a breath and turned his way. Another woman had just approached and leaned into the man from where she stood on his other side. They kissed one another's cheeks before the woman settled onto the empty stool on that side of him. She was fiftyish, attractive, poised. Louise felt her brow knit. *Daughter, lover?*

She turned away and heard their intimate laugh. A slow chill spread through her as color rose up behind her ears. She bit her lip, closed her eyes, made a tiny shake of her head. Quickly, she signed her receipt, took her credit card, and tossed back the rest of her wine. Then she slipped the credit card and leftover box into her purse, shrugged her sweater over her shoulders, and left without a glance towards the couple on the adjacent stools.

Outside, the gloaming had fallen fully, streetlights had come on, and a marine layer drifted in off the bay. Louise scowled. *What a fool you are. What were you thinking?* In spite of the crowded sidewalk and the familiar creak in her hip, she didn't slow her pace.

At the corner, she waited for the crosswalk signal to change next to a small boy holding his mother's hand. The boy squinted up at her while the signal's display counted down several seconds before saying, "Why are you crying?"

"I'm not," Louise managed.

She straightened, swallowed once, set her jaw, and fixed her eyes on the display's diminishing numbers, starting across alone before they reached "0". Once on the other side, Louise forced herself to think of the things that awaited her in the condo. Her orchids were due watering, there was a movie she'd DVR'd that she could watch, the bed linens needed changing.

But there were no children to call, no family to contact, she'd made no friends yet nearby with whom to get in touch. Just a lovely and well-appointed second-floor condo filled with a silence that seemed to sometimes scream but on whose tiny balcony overlooking the bay she often sat with her coffee or a sandwich or a glass of wine and thought about things as time, like sand in an hourglass, slip-slip-slipped away.

Photography – B. Carroll

Thomas Penn Johnson
Vicarage

For the first time in their young lives three friends, street urchins in the main, all had jobs, at the university; had obtained together their first apartment and were about to receive their first official visitor.

Wally, at nineteen, was the oldest, and the apartment was officially in his name. Orphaned at seventeen, he and his sister Cindy, three years younger than he, had attempted unsuccessfully to make it, bouncing haphazardly from one ramshackle slum dwelling to another for the past two years. Cindy was now living with an ill-tempered and parsimonious aunt, kind enough to take in her dead brother's desperate girl but adamant in her refusal to take in the boy she considered grown enough to take care of himself.

Thanks to the intervention of Vicar Larry Hubbard, assigned to the university chapel and a volunteer at the neighborhood youth center, Wally and his younger friend Louie had gotten work at the university cafeteria and secured an apartment on the second floor of a nice wood-frame house on College Avenue just two blocks from the university campus, two blocks distance from the youth center.

Kenny was only seventeen, but he was a fixture up on the hill at the university. For two years he had been working in maintenance there and knew more about the lawn-cutting and snow-plowing equipment than anyone else in maintenance. Everyone on the hill—students, faculty, and townspeople—recognized the affable, long-haired, blue-eyed, blond Kenny, seemingly ubiquitous around the campus winter and summer. He, too, was something of a rolling stone. Though his parents rented a decent place up on the hill, his father's alcohol addiction and violent temper made home barely habitable for his long-suffering mother and totally unendurable for their son. Kenny spent most of his non-working hours at the youth center; and, ever since Vicar Hubbard came to town Kenny had simply insinuated himself into the Vicar's orbit.

Louie was the youngest and the smallest of the three roommates, though none of the friends was more than one hundred and fifty pounds, or taller than 5'9". Of necessity, they were all roguish to some degree, Kenny being an out-and-out playboy and *bon vivant*.

What distinguished Louie from his peers was stunning beauty and aura of angelic charm. A casual observer would take him to be quiet and soft-spoken, and no moderately perceptive eyes would miss the natural twinkle in his dark brown eyes, the striking depth of the dimple in his right cheek, or the darkly lugubrious shadow cast over his person by his gloriously long eyelashes and mane of reddish-brown hair. All this was punctuated by well-formed biceps and powerful legs. Louie was born and raised in Kentucky but lived for the last year in Indiana, his divorced mother's birthplace. Bluntly put, Wally was rather plain though by no means unattractive, but dark-haired Louie and fair-haired Kenny together were a vision of loveliness from out of this world.

When Larry Hubbard received the rare vicarage assignment to a campus ministry, all at the seminary regarded it as most fortuitous. Indeed, it was the only vicarage he had aspired to, having concluded back in his sophomore year that the parish ministry suited neither his liberal social attitudes nor his scholar's predilections. Never had he expected, however, when he sought to broaden his secular social service experiences by volunteering to do counseling at the youth center, that he would fall inexplicably in love with the street urchins he would meet there, especially Kenny. Through Kenny he had become friends with Louie, Wally, and a host of others, several of whom in due course educated him to the fact that, as one of them put it: *You are one of us now!*

Yet, as he walked on a warm Saturday evening the blocks from the youth center to the College Avenue apartment of his friends, Larry Hubbard knew that the occasion was no mere happenstance. In a sense, the Vicar had been the moving party to the apartment acquisition:

without him Louie and Wally would have no cafeteria jobs, and it was doubtful that old Mrs. Strietelmeier would have consented to rent her upstairs to the three roommates, two of whom had not reached their majority. Even after a long day of work at the university chapel and at the youth center, Vicar Hubbard walked deliberately, buoyed by the newly awakened satisfaction of his going to visit Kenny at *his* place.

When Kenny opened the apartment door he should have expected Larry to be there, but he reflexively darted his eyes back inside in a manner that looked to the Vicar much like a game-warden throwing a protective glance around his warren. *It's Larry!* Kenny says, instinctively, to the room.

There was no mistaking the delight overtaking Kenny's visage when he looked back to the Vicar. When their eyes met and locked on, they were swept away by a tsunami of friendship love to their own sacred island where only true friends can go.

You guys going to invite me in or not?

Wally and Louie immediately appear beside Kenny, and the three roommates join in a chorus of sincere welcome: *What took you so long? Please come in! You the Man!*

Now there were four men joined in an intimacy akin to that of a "circle jerk," each one feeling mounting ecstasy as the roommates proudly showed off their new place to their adored benefactor. The Vicar was overjoyed to see how well appointed the place was after barely a week of occupancy; he became so excited when they finished their tour that had his sense of propriety permitted, he would have embraced each of them then and there, but consciously restraining himself he extended his hand to each for a vigorous handshake. To the Vicar's surprise Louie, wet-eyed and speechless, would not release the Vicar's hand, and with his unbelievably soft hand gently turned the Vicar's over first one way and then back again. Overwhelmed in these uncharted waters, the Vicar pulled the lad to himself for an embrace so intense and innocent that neither man took any note of the swelling passion they felt between them.

Wally had plans for the night, so he was the first to excuse himself: *Cindy's coming over tonight, she's gonna make spaghetti for everybody tomorrow; so I have to head out to get her.* It turned out that Louie also needed to go out to see about getting a stereo, so the Vicar decided to leave at the same time as the others, and Kenny offered to walk him part way home.

On that walk Kenny gingerly broached a subject he was loath to bring up:

There's something I have to tell you. I don't like it, and I am sure you won't either. Half that stuff you saw in our apartment—lamps and dishes and silverware and the corn plant and aloes-thing-- well, Louie and Wally stole all that stuff from the campus!

What? exclaims Vicar Hubbard. *What!* he repeats.

Stole it. All week long, every night. And don't ask me where Louie plans to get the stereo he says he's going to get. I didn't have anything to do with any of it!

His good spirits now abashed, Vicar Hubbard thanked Kenny for telling him and told his friend that he would come over after church the next day to set things right. During the solitary portion of his walk home Vicar Hubbard had a lot to sort out. Hard as it was to process the consuming feeling of betrayal he could not deny, he thought he could comprehend Wally's situation. Wally was a son of destitution and desperation who undoubtedly was operating according to the morality of destitution.

The Vicar understood poverty, having himself been the child of a single mother from the ghetto, and he was street savvy enough to recognize that the destitute lived more than a notch or two below the rank of merely poor, in a desperate place beyond his capacity to comprehend. He reckoned that the morality of destitution was no reflection on the character of its practitioners; rather, it was simply a given, a serendipitous happenstance of existence. Searching his mind and heart, he concluded that he believed that Wally was a good soul, with a good heart, and that with a heartfelt admonition Wally would be the sort who could see the errors of his ways and mend his ways.

But Louie was another matter. The Vicar knew the boy's innate tenderness and the mesmerizing strength of his carriage; he had just that evening experienced the seductive magic of his powerful passions. But he also knew that although his parents were divorced and that his father lived far away in Paducah, Kentucky,

Louie's hard-working family was neither destitute nor disposed to commit crimes.

The Vicar had no idea what was the basis of Louie's dishonesty. The next day, when the Vicar arrived at the apartment on College Avenue, he found Wally and Kenny in a state of high panic. During the night, Louie had been apprehended breaking into a frat house and was even then incarcerated in the county jail. This news catapulted the Vicar into pastoral urgent mode: he was a shepherd with a lost sheep, determined to save his flock. to use this occasion as an opportunity to turn a lost lamb around. Anticipating an arraignment hearing for a juvenile on Monday, Vicar Hubbard spent the rest of the day conferring with Dennis Morgan, the director of the youth center who had some clout with the prosecutor's office, and consoling Louie's worried mother and friends, including a terrified Cindy who, unbeknownst to anyone besides her aunt, was pregnant with Louie's baby.

On Monday morning when Larry arrived at the courthouse, coincidentally at the same time as several of Louie's young admirers and worried friends, the closed hearing was already begun, but Larry Hubbard was pleased to assure all waiting in the hallway that he and Dennis Morgan had worked out an agreement with the prosecutors that Louie would be paroled to the supervision of his mother and the youth center, and at worst he might get weekends in the county lockup but be able to keep his job and apartment. And the Vicar was elated to learn from the bailiff that Louie's father had flown up from Paducah, fortunately making both mother and father present at the hearing.

What was not known to Vicar Hubbard and some of Louie's young associates assembled in the hall was that Louie was a pot-smoking, marijuana-dealing run-away from the home of his dictatorial and abusive father, a sheriff's deputy in Paducah, who had legal custody of the boy. When the doors of the hearing room finally opened there was a pliant Louie, hands handcuffed behind his back, tears streaming from his eyes. The father had demanded that the boy receive no probation and be remanded to jail in order that he might learn to submit to authority.

Looking straight into Louie's eyes, Vicar Hubbard saw there what he himself felt—betrayal, annihilation, utter defeat. There before him stood the closest approximation he could imagine to spectacularly beautiful Lucifer plummeting headlong through Chaos.

Patty Somlo
What Is Lost

This is not a piece about cancer. No one, including me, cares to read that. Instead, I want to share a bit of what gets lost when the person you most love becomes ill with a serious, terminal disease.

If friends were asked to describe Richard's and my life, they would surely start with hiking, and travel to rustic, beautiful spots. Since Richard's diagnosis with stage four cancer four years ago, when we lost the easy ability to pick up and go, our hiking boots, sticks, and inflatable blue and white kayak filling the car, we have often reminisced about that life. On our first date, Richard and I had taken the ferry from Tiburon to Angel Island, a short distance across San Francisco Bay. After reaching the island, he and I did something we would repeat as often as possible for the next nearly thirty years—we climbed a narrow dusty trail, found a place to sit and enjoy the view, and talked.

Some hikes we took were long, others short. Favorite trails never grew old. The best ones provided views of lakes, peaks, or the ocean, and led to spectacular spots for lunch.

Before meeting Richard, I had been single for years. Finally having a companion to travel to places where walking could take me to mountain lakes or wildflower-strewn meadows seemed like a dream. Richard had done some backpacking and camping with his previous wife. But in our early days, he wasn't quite fit for the uphill treks I enjoyed. I worked to change that.

Once an avid photographer, Richard had given up that beloved hobby years before. He had served as his high school photographer, running around school gyms to capture the moment a member of the team made a great shot. At the same time, he photographed his parents' friends and relatives at parties, developing black and white negatives in the bathroom, then making prints and selling them to the guests.

Early on, we started leaving the city for long weekends and vacations, where people were far outnumbered by trees. Each morning during one stay in Big Sur on the Central California Coast, we stepped out of our log cabin and took seats on large boulders next to the Big Sur River, to enjoy our coffee, along with the glorious view. The last morning of that trip, Richard realized he wanted to start photographing again, to be able to take that sight of sunlight sparkling on water back home with him.

Now, Richard had more motivation to get up those steep trails, anticipating memorable photographs he wouldn't get elsewhere. We climbed trails in Yosemite, Glacier, Zion, Bryce, and Mount Rainier National Parks. During the twelve years we lived in Portland, Oregon, we trekked to myriad waterfalls in the nearby Columbia Gorge and hiked around splendid lakes and alongside rushing streams at Mount Hood. In Eastern Oregon, we explored the colorful splendor of the John Day Fossil Beds Monument, while spending nights in Mitchell, a tiny remote village in which nearly every building on the one downtown street was for sale.

And we went to Hawaii. I can still picture Richard's astonished face as he slipped on a wet rock and dropped into a stream we were attempting to cross, along the Kalalau Trail, located on Kauai's spectacular Nepali Coast.

Four and a half years ago, we finally made it to Southern Utah, a place we had yearned to visit for decades. We followed trails in magical Bryce Canyon and marveled at the moonscape-like formations as we hiked in the Grand Staircase-Escalante National Monument.

One month after we returned home, Richard started experiencing severe back pain. Several months later when we learned the cause—metastatic cancer, we cried. Neither of us knew a thing about cancer. Being the least optimistic, I assumed Richard was about to die. Thankfully, I was wrong.

What we have learned these four years is that while stage four cancer is treatable (but not curable), the treatment and the disease take a toll. Bit by bit, the chemotherapy keeping my husband alive has stolen pieces of his life.

Even so, for the longest time, when he got a break from the every three-weeks' treatments, he was still able to hike. The week of our anniversary, we headed back to a favorite spot, Graeagle, California, at the edge of the Lakes Basin Recreation Area. By then, the treatment had slowed Richard down, and we feared a favorite hike probably would be too hard.

The hike we normally took to lovely, serene Silver Lake, where we enjoyed sitting on the bank to eat lunch, had a string of perfect lakes along the way. We assumed Richard couldn't get all the way to Silver, but thought he might make it as far as Big Lake, about a mile and a half up.

There wasn't a cloud in the sky, the air at that higher elevation pure and fresh. We walked slowly up the rocky trail, with me leading the way. From time to time, I turned around, to make sure Richard was doing okay, and backtracked if I'd gone too far.

When we reached the shore of Big Lake, with reflections of trees mirrored across the still surface, Richard smiled and lifted the camera hanging from a strap around his neck to his eye. We noted, as we always did on hikes, the stunning scenery. At that point, I assumed we'd find a rock or log to rest, then make our way back down to the car.

Then Richard surprised me and said, "Let's keep going. I feel all right."

So, we kept on, our pace more measured than in the past, but heading uphill all the same.

The tuna sandwiches I'd made that morning tasted like gourmet fare. Sitting on our favorite boulders, on the shore of Silver Lake, with a view of the silver-blue water and the Sierra Buttes beyond, Richard and I felt we'd been given a gift, more precious because it had been unexpected.

That was our last hike to Silver Lake, and our final Graeagle stay.

Richard might have reached Big Lake, and perhaps even Silver, the following year. But Covid-19 made the trip impossible. The next year, I secured a reservation to coincide with our anniversary, at a vacation rental with a wonderful view of Mill Pond. We had stayed there two years before, and the pond was glorious from first light until dusk. Early mornings, mist hovered low over the water, occasionally broken by a flock of Canadian geese lifting into the air. As the sun came up, the gray-white mist turned shades of pink and orange, eventually drifting away.

Several weeks before we were to arrive, a wildfire started in a remote forested area nearby. I checked the CalFire reports each day, seeing the Dixie Fire expand and edge closer to where we planned to stay. Living in an area of Northern California that has experienced devastating wildfires in recent years, I understood that even if the fire stayed far away from Graeagle, the dark choking smoke would not. I rescheduled for later in the fall.

But luck was not with us then. My husband's cancer had spread. The week we'd reserved, he needed to be in a clinic for specialized treatment.

I take daily walks now, mostly around my neighborhood. Streets and sidewalks are level, so Richard occasionally comes along. He leans on the same walking stick he has used to steady himself on rocky and slippery trails, from Kauai's Nepali Coast to the Pacific Crest Trail in Central Oregon. His feet have grown numb from chemotherapy, which affects his balance. Our pace is generally slow.

A terminal illness such as stage four cancer takes abilities away, piece by precious piece. For my husband, a landscape photographer and lover of the outdoors, the experience of being in wilderness areas, where beauty appears untouched, has been lost. Our life together has been spent hiking up or down mountains, paddling around lakes or down rivers, sitting on a bank eating lunch, or celebrating a memorable hike with floats and shakes at a favorite mountain town spot. What is lost can only be measured in tears shed from time to time.

Much as the dense fog obscured our path one August day on Mt. Tamalpais, the rough journey we have been on these past four years doesn't have a clear way forward. What is lost from an active life intimately connected to nature, though, is clear. At the same time, what remains—through memories, stories, experience and lessons learned—isn't easily dismissed. Nor are Richard's scores of oft-exhibited photographs, including those taken with one of his medium-format cameras of snow-covered Mt. Rainier, that capture both the stunning landscapes and how those places made the photographer feel.

On this painful cancer journey, I have learned that grieving is necessary, but also letting in gratefulness and joy. Many people, I remind Richard, never have the opportunities we have had to visit and hike and see so many wondrous sites. I have stores of memories, including walking a trail in the dark, unbroken by artificial light, to witness the Kilauea Volcano on the Big Island of Hawaii, spew liquid lava and orange fire toward the sky. It is best, I know, not to dwell on what has been lost, but instead to be thankful for a life filled with love, for one another and this earth we've done our best to appreciate, in all its unforgettable splendor.

Photography - D Ferrara

Burt Rashbaum
What the Next Day Would Bring

She didn't know the couple well. She'd met them a couple of times, saw how close the husbands were, like brothers, having grown up together, as comfortable in each other's houses as they were in their own. When they'd had their son, she sent them a gift and hoped the two families would grow together, get to know each other better, create happy memories.

When she met her husband her son was young, and she worried that once he found out she was a mom, he'd walk. But he right then expressed an interest in meeting her boy.

"He's an extension of you," he said, "so if he doesn't like me, what are my chances?"

Her son took to him right away. On their third date, which he insisted include her son, he volunteered to read to him as part of the pre-sleep ritual. In the living room she listened as he read story after story. There'd been laughter, then she heard him say, "How many stories does your mom usually read to you?" She smiled at his answer, "One."

"So," he said, "you're taking advantage of my not knowing that!"

"What's taking advantage?" he'd asked.

They were married three months later. Her son walked her down the aisle, he moved into their place, and suddenly they were a family. They had a comfortable love, he seemed like a missing puzzle piece that fit right into where he belonged.

The years slipped by, her son grew, and her husband truly became a father to her boy. Their boy. Maybe because her son was so young when she married, he'd started calling him 'Dad' right away. She'd heard about her husband's best friend for so long before the two couples met that she felt it couldn't have been their first meeting. Their two boys got along so well. She found it a bit disconcerting when this couple's son called her husband 'Uncle,' but found out later that he'd always been thought of as a brother to her husband's friend, so suddenly she was 'Aunt,' and the two boys became faux cousins. The two families didn't see each other much, but whenever they did it was natural, easy fun.

Now their son was entering high school. She tried to be in a place of gratitude every night as she drifted off to sleep, and one such night thanking her lucky stars, the phone rang. Her husband, fading to sleep, reached over and picked it up and said to her, half in jest, "Someone died," because who else would it be?

He said hello and then suddenly sat up, the phone to his ear. They were both instantly alert, awake. He was on the phone for a long time. Finally he hung up.

"What?" she said.

"An accident," he said, "a terrible...I gotta go."

He grabbed his pants and was gone before she could ask another question. She tried to read, she tried TV, but finally gave up and sat in the kitchen, waiting.

When his car pulled in, she took a breath and knew that whatever he was dealing with, she would accept it, and be strong.

She expected him to come in, sit down, and tell her the story of whatever the accident was, why he'd had to leave. The door opened, and she heard not one, but two sets of footsteps. Her husband said, "There's a bed in the spare room, you go to sleep and we'll talk in the morning," and that second set of steps slowly trudged up the stairs.

He appeared in the kitchen doorway, and looked like a little boy who'd been crying for hours.

"What?" she said, going to him.

"They're gone," he said, and broke down in her arms.

She led him to the table, waited for him to collect himself. Their friends had been killed in a car wreck. Their son had been home. Her husband's friend had no family, he'd been an only child, like her husband, like her own son, their son. The wife had no close family. She found out, for the first time, that her husband and his best friend had discussed such a situation, and their wills had specified that if either couple were ever to meet an untimely death, the surviving couple would adopt the surviving son and raise him as their own.

She didn't know any of this. She looked at the ceiling, knowing the poor boy was up there, his life torn to shreds, probably in shock.

Her husband wept quietly.

"We have to take him," he said, wiping his eyes. "He's lost. He's broken. But he's ours now."

"But," she didn't know what to say, or even what to think, "but how?"

"I don't know," he said. "But this is the way it is."

She kissed him and stood. He looked at her with questions in his eyes. "Come to bed when you're ready," she said.

She slowly walked up the stairs, and with every step she felt their previous life slip away. When she got to the top of the landing everything felt different. She headed down the hall, took her new son in her arms, and let him cry until he was spent. Then she laid his head down on the pillow, stood there until he was asleep, and had no idea what the next day would bring.

Photography – B. Carroll

Don Noel
Orchestral Passions

Priscilla had looked forward to this all week, yet now felt vaguely uncomfortable. Residual pandemic caution? Let go, she told herself; spring has sprung; enjoy it!

The familiar gilded proscenium arch framing the stage should have been reassuring. Poor Howard would have enjoyed this return to almost-normalcy. The last time they'd come, before he fell ill, he'd liked being chauffeured in Harmony Acres' comfortable bus, after years of hoofing through the vast parking lot. Tonight, they would have been allowed to sit together, even hold hands. Most of her neighbors had a vacant seat on either side in compliance with the latest limited-occupancy regimen, but were a good deal less than six feet apart.

Maybe that's what made her uncomfortable? Too close to people taking off their masks? That's silly, Priscilla; everyone's had their shots and boosters, or they wouldn't be allowed in. She turned to the program: a concert performance of the opera "Salomé," an old favorite.

When the chattering instruments fell silent, she looked up to see the concertmaster tuck his violin under his chin and wait for the oboe's concert pitch. Then the usual cacophony as all instruments played that note, some playing a scale, too. Ah, tradition! Like prayer before meals, Howard had liked to say: Probably unnecessary, but made everything taste better.

She felt disappointed not to see the oboist. Pandemic-long she'd been "streaming" concerts—whatever that meant—and cameras always showed the woodwinds at this opening moment. Might the oboist be a woman, in this new liberated world, the tune-the-orchestra barrier breached in her hometown?

And now the soloists paraded in, both men and women in chiaroscuro except for Salomé in a flame-red gown with seductive expanses of shoulder. They took off masks and bowed, joined by the conductor. Good thing the orchestra pit stood between them and the audience, Priscilla thought: Health experts said singers expelled droplets like tiny rainstorms. Doctor Fauci still advised maintaining the protective regimen in crowds.

She made herself concentrate on the music. The captain of the guard sang, *Wie schön ist die Prinzessin Salomé.* Priscilla remembered: He was lusting after Salomé. He wasn't quite acting, but gave it some body language and facial expression.

This whole opera was about lust, she thought. The guardsman lusted after Salomé; her stepfather Herod, who would sing soon, lusted after her too. But she ignored them and lusted after Jochanaan, John the Baptist, imprisoned in a well almost offstage. In a deep-in-a-well baritone he prophesized the coming of Christ and condemned all the lusting.

Priscilla wondered if her granddaughters, away now at college, were into lusting yet.

The princess had Jochanaan brought up from the well, and lusted after him in good voice and extravagant detail. Priscilla longed for subtitles. I've been spoiled by watching the world on the tube, she thought.

This Salomé was a handsome woman; *zaftig*, Howard might have said, slyly whisper-translating for his wife: "stacked." But she shouldn't be much older than the grands. Last week, home on vacation, they'd taken her to lunch in a thinly-populated restaurant with tables partitioned like eggs in a carton.

Imagine, a year-plus without seeing your grandchildren! Hardly conducive to sharing intimate growing-up thoughts like whether they were in love, let alone lust. Everyone at Harmony Acres was presumably well past most lusting, but the recent news had been full of important people lusting after the wrong people.

She let her mind wander over the terrain of desire while the orchestra and singers worked at Richard Strauss's raucous score. Then the piccolo or flute offered the *leitmotif* of Salomé's passion. The newer generation wore their musical themes on their sleeves and succumbed to passion uninhibited; she wondered if that made their lives less complicated than in her day. Her granddaughters had made their lives sound improbably uncomplicated.

On stage, lust was certainly making life complicated. *"Wie schön ist die Prinzessen Salomé,"* Herod sang, the very words the guardsman had used. Priscilla sympathized with Herodias: With her new husband telling the world that he lusted after her daughter, Herodias was understandably not in a good mood, and Strauss hadn't given her much melody.

Herod paid no attention to his wife; Salomé was offering a bargain. If he would grant her any wish, she would dance for him. Priscilla hoped they might actually perform the dance of the seven veils, which Howard once called the most demure strip tease in stage history.

No such luck: Salomé only shimmied, a primly operatic bump-and-grind; but the orchestra played it well. And now here she was naming her price: *"in einer Silberschussel. . ."*

The old lecher was eager to please: "Yes, yes, what do you want on your silver platter?"

"Den Kopf des Jochanaan." Give me his head.

She and Howard had seen a full operatic version long ago when a much-too-realistic prophet's head was brought up on a silver tray; Salomé's kiss had been repulsive. In this sterile setting, the soprano mimed it inoffensively, and one could concentrate on the music.

And then bang! It was over: Herod had his soldiers crush her with their shields, an outburst of instrumental discord. Then a moment's total silence as the audience took in the suddenness of Salomé's demise.

It had been spellbinding. Priscilla would have joined in a standing ovation, but her carefully spaced neighbors were more sedate. It takes a full house, shoulder-to-shoulder, to whip up real jubilation, she thought, as when the college basketball women won a title game on television the other night: This audience couldn't make enough noise. Finally she turned to follow the others up the aisle. Soon she could take those grands to a concert.

No, not both at once. Next time she would invite them singly. Intimacy amidst a crowd would be special: Each young woman whispering to her ancient grandmother the secrets of her heart— emotions and compulsions that moved people long before Strauss put them to music.

Post-pandemic passion. Something to look forward to.

J. Alan Nelson
Stars Die

The Universe is disappearing, and there's nothing we can do about it.
-Ethan Siegel

The universe disappears. Many of those stars we see at night died before we came here. So. So? Words written by people long dead still live: Jane Austen, Socrates, Homer, Dante, and Douglas Adams shine so bright. Yep. I love Trillian with a heat so fierce I'm frightened. I dislike Uriah Heep with such bitter horror I'm easily capable of violence. I still smile as the number 42 inevitably pops up, a fuck-you answer to this disturbing universe. Dante may rescue Virgil from Hell, but Virgil rescued himself with his story of Paris fleeing to found Rome. Mercutio's senseless death breaks my heart, then breaks it again. And again. The loneliness of Huck Finn on that river raft flows into a flood. Yes I love facts like 95 percent of the galaxies in the known universe are unreachable. Yes, I watch the light brighten and fade every day, eight minutes from its source. The universe disappears. We are desperate creatures who understand our universe will disappear. Any mark we make, any child of a child of a child will not survive. No one will care about the marks on my thumb made by a rattlesnake forty years ago. Or the bullet scar on my calf by a clumsy airport security guard. I did not survive the snake and the bullet only to die a futile death. Yes. I do not merely survive. Yes. I feel sadness rise like a wave. I must surf the wave or be crushed. So do I end this futile life now, not participate in this existential nonsense? Or do I live live live to fight the fiery entropy spewed by Beowulf's dragon? I know all falls apart. I know I die, decay or burn. But I come from exploded stars with ancient atoms that vibrate with electrons that jolt electric as Thor's hammer. A fool I may be. A fool who whistles in the dark. A fool who must shout words into the unknown. What mind will these words strike, flame into a brilliance that surprises us all?

Cindy Pope
That Damned Blue Dress

In the heat and humidity of that day in May, I looked like I had just stepped out of the shower. But that didn't matter because I got asked out for my first car date. That meant a movie at the only theater in my small Southern town, and a trip to the Pizza Hut, the only restaurant where a teenager could afford to take a date. I had just turned fifteen, and my date, Mike, an upperclassman, bore a vague resemblance to Ritchie Cunningham of *Happy Days*. He and I had known each other since we were five and four years old, the one reason my mom agreed to let me go.

Mom stipulated that I had to be home by 10:00. She also made us have another couple with us. We ended up double dating with his older step-brother, Ricky, and Ricky's girlfriend, Brenda.

My big day arrived. I half-heartily did my Saturday housecleaning chores with images of my night with Mike playing in my head. I finished in time to paint my nails and re-read the latest editions of *Teen Beat* and *Tiger Beat* magazines cover to cover . . . again. Once my nails were dry enough, I laid out my jeans, t-shirt, and sandals on the side of the bed; and went to take a bath.

I came out of the bathroom with my hair twisted in a towel and searched for my good underwear, but something wasn't right. I turned to the bed. My jeans and t-shirt were gone. In their place lay a Sunday dress, slip, and panty hose. In the floor beside my bed, a pair of navy heels caught my eye. I shuddered at the thought of wearing panty hose and heels in the late afternoon heat and humidity.

What the . . .? Anger swelled through me while I jammed my arms through the sleeves of my robe. My fingers shook while I tried tying the sash. Then I stomped off to find Mom.

When I asked what happened to the clothes I had laid out, she turned around and glared. "You're not going to the new movie theatre dressed like a tramp! I would hate to think what Mike's mother would think when he told her that I let you leave the house dressed like a floozy."

"But everyone else is going to be in jeans and t-shirt!" The thought of having to walk from the parking lot to the front of the theatre where my new high school friends gathered made me sick to my stomach.

"No, they're not. They are going to know that you are a decent young lady who knows how to dress for a date." She turned her back, letting me know the conversation had come to a close.

But I wasn't going to let it go. "Yeah, right." I choked back the tears.

"You'll see. When Mike comes to the door and he's dressed nice, you'll be the one looking like a fool in sloppy jeans and an old t-shirt."

"No, I'm going to look like a fool dressed like I'm going to church. Everyone is going to make fun of me." I turned to leave but stopped and whirled around. "And just so you know, the *new* movie theatre hasn't been *new* for years."

She pointed her forefinger at me. "Keep it up, and *you* won't go. Period."

"But I'm telling you that everyone else—"

"I don't care what everyone else does. *You* are going to dress like you are somebody!"

We argued until I was going to be late. And I still had to figure out the best way to style my long, stringy brown hair so it would cover the pimple that had had all week to disappear.

Mom followed me into my room to "help" me dress. I'm sure she just wanted to make sure I didn't sneak out in another pair of jeans and t-shirt.

I really didn't dislike the dress. In fact, the fashionable cut flattered my figure, and the light blue enhanced my skin tone and matched my eyes. It had little red, yellow, and green embroidered flowers across the top for contrast, and the short, puffy sleeves made it rather cute.

Mom had the last hank of my hair wrapped around the curling iron in a useless attempt to get my hair to defy the law of humidity, when Mike knocked on the front door.

I rushed to open it, with mom close behind.

There stood Mike in jeans and t-shirt. I glanced over his shoulder, and from the open door I could see Ricky and Brenda in the front seat of the car. Also in t-shirts.

I stood there in a church dress, panty hose, and heels. Mike's expression changed from one of delight to sheer embarrassment when he saw me.

Blood rushed through my cheeks to my hairline. I wanted to crawl into a hole and pull it in after me. But by then, there was no time for me to change.

Mom asked about Brenda and what we were going to see, going on and on like we had all the time in the world. Before we got out the door, she reminded him loudly of my 10:00 curfew.

From the front porch, I saw Ricky and Brenda laughing. Mike and I glanced at each other, knowing the movie started at seven, which didn't leave much time for pizza after the movie, much less parking at the lake.

"Y'all have a good time," Mom laughed. "But not too good of a time."

Dear God, just shoot me now!

Once I heard the front door close, I breathed a little easier. I planned to enjoy the next few precious hours of freedom ahead of me.

At the theatre, I had to walk through the steaming hot parking lot dressed for a wedding (or a funeral, the way I felt), and up the sidewalk, and wait outside for Mike and Ricky to purchase our movie tickets.

High schoolers swarmed the whole area. All were wearing jeans and t-shirts. All were staring at me.

Thank goodness no one could see my dress in the dark theater.

For a couple of hours I forgot about the damned thing. I have no idea which movie we saw or who starred in it, but I do remember Mike kissed me a couple of times, and we held hands through most of the show.

After the movie, thank God the sun had almost set and no one paid any attention to my bright blue frock. While Ricky drove us the half mile to Pizza Hut, Mike and I sat in the back seat and held hands.

Under the bright lights of the restaurant, there was no hiding the fact that my bright blue dress stuck out worse than the pimple on my forehead.

Brenda sat across from me, with her perfect complexion, long, straight, magazine-cover blonde hair, never a strand out of place, and wearing the cutest little cut-off baseball-style t-shirt that brushed the top of her hip-hugger jeans. There I sat feeling like a complete idiot all dressed up for a Sunday morning sermon.

Because she was an upper classman, I didn't know Brenda well, and I didn't know Ricky at all. But being older and sophisticated, they were so cool and in-the-know about all the newest fads, happenings at school and around town, concerts, and which kids put on the best drinking parties.

I watched the three of them talk and laugh and cut-up while my nervous stomach rumbled and grumbled. Each time I tried to make whip-smart snappy comebacks, my words came out sounding stupid. Way out of my depth and embarrassed as hell, I inched myself into the corner crevice of the booth.

When the waitress brought the two large pizzas to our table, Mike loaded my plate with a huge slice and placed it in front of me. "Here, eat up."

My stomach rolled at the smell of tomato sauce. I closed my eyes against the disgusting globs of grease sitting on top of the cheese. I sipped on the large Coke, which somewhat settled my nervous stomach. I managed to eat half a slice, and prayed the whole time I wouldn't get sick.

Poor Mike had to eat most of the pie by himself.

By the time I began to feel somewhat comfortable around them, Mike looked at his watch, reminding Ricky about my curfew. Ricky drove us back to my house with seconds to spare.

Mike and I held hands while he walked me to the door. Mom had left the porch light on, and everyone on the block could see everything. While Mike and I chatted and flirted, Ricky and Brenda were making out in the front seat of his land-yacht of a car.

Then the front porch light flickered.

Mike laughed. "That your signal?"

Once again, I wanted to die. "I suppose so." I'm not sure what mom thought we were doing out there, because I'm so short that while I stood at the edge of the porch, Mike stood on the step below so we could be eye to eye.

After more flirting and kissing, we couldn't ignore the lights flickering again.

Dear God, please help me!

"Guess I'd better go." He chuckled.

I sighed. "I guess so."

He kissed me one last time and turned toward the car, coughing to make sure Ricky and Brenda heard him approach. While I fumbled for my keys, he turned back. "Oh, and by the way." His voice carried in the still of the night.

"Yes?"

"Next time, how about wearing jeans and t-shirt? Okay?"

With one hand propped on the front door, I said, louder than I intended, "Hey." I gestured at my dress. "*This* was NOT my idea!"

With that, the front door flew open, and I fell off my heels and landed face first at my mom's feet.

"Did you have a good time?"

"Swell." Sarcasm poured through every pore of my body. I picked myself up, jerked the hem of my dress back down to cover my good underwear, kicked the shoes off, and stomped to my bedroom. "And by the way, you did see what Mike, Ricky, and Brenda were wearing, right?"

Mom sighed. "Yes. You were right, and I'm sorry.

But I saw a grin spread across her face.

Image - D Ferrara

Tim Walker
The Ancient Widower

Our families only knew our wedding day from photographs, so after your memorial I take your sisters and your favorite niece on a tour, the small wedding album in hand. We stand in the courthouse garden, on the spot where we were married, now hemmed in by strangers' weddings, with large wedding parties and many guests. None has picked our spot, leaving it free for us.

Just here we stood and faced the judge, the Maid of Honor beaming as we said our vows. Only it's been so long, I can't always tell real memories from those constructed from the Best Man's photos. Trees have grown, but the buildings haven'tchanged: white stucco and red tile, triumphant archways, small windows set deep in the walls, barred with scrolling ironwork. And you, so stylish, so skilled with your fingers, wore the dress you made, and I in my corduroy jacket and tan slacks, my side-parted hair already morphed into a comb-over that flopped on my forehead. A moment frozen, forever fresh, if somewhat two-dimensional.

We follow the album's trail to the top of the courthouse tower, where we posed in shade with bright foothills behind. We admire the view in four directions, wait for a turn at the rail where newlyweds and their guests line up and vie for space to make their own mementos.

I can see myself stopping one of three wedding guests with my wrinkled claw and fix him with a glittering eye, and tell the tale of my love and sorrow, and give him something else to think about. But—what if he should he panic and cry out,

Hold off! unhand me grey-beard loon!

I don't want to make a scene, so I desist and we pass on together.

We follow the album across town, and view from the street our first rental, the site of our reception, where friends stood by tensely when we fed each other cake, then chilled when they saw us do it nicely.

Next morning, we sat by the kitchen window with our coffee and watched the towhees scratching breakfast in the duff.

D Ferrara
Arms Raised in America*

Worst storm to hit the Midwest in almost twenty years, the radio said. Twenty years ago, she had been living in New York. She did still. The Midwest was a dimly realized concept having something to do with cows. Cornfields.

Her flight had been diverted two hundred miles from where she needed to be. Barely able to see through the windshield, she had driven madly for five hours before her cell phone found service, a few miles from her meeting. The message: meeting cancelled, with not even an apology for her wasted trip.

She pulled to what she hoped was the side of the road, hazard lights ticking. Resting her forehead on the steering wheel, she listened to the rain clattering over the car, tallying up the costs: So many drops for airfare, the rented car, the hotel room, missed opportunities elsewhere... Time. Lost. Useless.

Somehow, she found her hotel. Without having ever been here, she knew the rooms would have beige walls, a hunter green and burgundy bedspread, a too small desk, a too hard chair, rubbery pillows. Faint whiff of must. A room with anywhere outside and nowhere within.

All this was a reminder that the promise of clean sheets had replaced the spirit of discovery, as if the point of travel was not to experience the new but to recreate the old again and again.

―――――――――――――――――――――

*Originally published in *Amarillo Bay.*

The apologetic desk clerk explained that the restaurant was closed because of the storm; he offered her cereal from the breakfast supplies in the lounge.

"Or," he said with a smile, "The Mall is still open."

She blinked.

He pulled out a glossy map with stores, restaurants, vendors on carts, movies, and "attractions" in its pleats. He pointed out the door to an enormous structure (revealed by a sudden flash of lightning), circling items on the map, describing with enthusiasm the wonders so close at hand.

She could park in The Wild West and be in the food court without going outside at all, the clerk gushed. When she hesitated, he confessed that housekeepers had not made it to work and he would have to make up her room.

She left her bags and headed for The Mall.

Inside was perpetually fluorescent day, punctuated faintly by an almost-regular clanking and other mechanical sounds. She found a directory listing stores and restaurants. Four Mexican. Three pizza. Burgers. The Korn Dog Palace. Sushi. *Sushi? No. Not here.*

On the map, The Mall was square, with layers of stores surrounding something called "The Great Plains." She was on New Orleans Jazz Way. "You Are Here" was opposite a food court.

She headed for the Great Plains. To her surprise, this was an amusement park. The mechanical sounds were rides—"attractions."

Buried in the innermost reaches of The Mall, the Great Plains was invisible even to its vast parking lots. Yet every ride was running, like carnivals in parking lots, flashing temporary pleasures to attract customers.

It wasn't helping.

The Plains reeked of frying food: donuts, funnel cakes, corn dogs, french fries. There were ice cream parlors, a "steakhouse," taco stands, chicken joints, cotton candy, soda, lemonade, face painting, and souvenirs. Remarkably fresh-faced young attendants in polo shirts proffered greasy tidbits.

That wasn't helping much either.

Over her head, roller coasters rushed. One, designed to resemble an old-fashioned train, clattered and clanked. The second, a sleeker, rocket shape, whooshed. For the third, single cars with four seats facing inward hurtled down metal slopes, tilting, pivoting around its center.

Far above, rain sheeted through the darkness onto a glass ceiling.

Some people had braved the Great Plains.

A lone man rode in the front of the train coaster, without expression, staring. Up the steep climb, along the edges, down the drops—he made no sound or gesture—crammed into his undersized seat.

Beneath him, a woman in tight pink capri pants and a pink cap set on fluffed, dyed-black hair passed. Heavily caked in a slightly wrong fleshtone, the woman strode on stiletto heels, shadowed by her miniature self: a tottering girl, also packed in makeup, clothes rhinestoned onto her thin frame. They stumbled towards the wildest of the roller coasters, with its spinning cars.

Their path was crossed by a phalanx of strollers—no, not strollers. Small wheelchairs, with pale children slumped, strapped. One child, androgynous, tufted blond, had a breathing tube. The fat, pale pushers wore professional indifference with their scrubs.

She averted her eyes.

She had not been to an amusement park since childhood. Some of the rides were familiar: the roller coasters, a huge Ferris wheel, a carousel. Others were frightening. "Axe": rows of seats, swung high and turned upside down, upending its two or three riders in padded harnesses. "Spider": eight huge arms spun wildly, holding small cages rotating in the opposite direction. "Kangaroo" dropped caged passengers down a pole, bumping along the way.

In the center were gentler treats—little trains, miniature roller coasters, bobbing balloons. Along the periphery: doors and caves, haunted houses, space trips, and cartoon adventures.

A group of girls with long wet skirts and hijabs rushed from the splashy log ride, anxious to ride again. Their attire would have raised no eyebrows in Beirut, though pure American giggles escaped the somber scarves. Several paused by a kiosk, laughing and pointing. A bank of screens showed photos of the riders, captured at harrowing points.

The cameras had caught the girls as the logs plunged down the steepest decline, some gripping safety bars or their scarves, as others raised their arms high, triumphant.

Past the photos was a sign, "Extreme Trampolines." As a child, she had loved the sensation of height and flight, jumping on beds and sofas until she grew too tall.

The trampolines were on an upper level, large black circles, each straddled by poles with long elastic ropes, like bungee cords.

"Am I too big?" she asked the smiling young man.

He was polite. "No, ma'am. The harnesses are weight-tested. You're plenty light."

She was grateful that he did not question why a middle-aged woman in a rumpled business suit would want to jump on a trampoline in a soggy Midwestern Mall.

"How much is it?"

"Three tickets."

"Oh," she said, "Tickets."

The young man shrugged. "Tell you what. If you want to jump, go ahead. I can't turn down my only customer after she's come out in this weather."

He helped her onto the trampoline and into the harness, clipping everything behind her back. He explained: the harness clamps could rotate freely as she jumped, allowing her to flip forward or back without missing the trampoline or hitting the edge.

For a minute, she stood, uncertain.

"It's okay," he encouraged, "just jump. You'll get the hang of it."

"How long do I have?"

He smiled broadly. "Ten minutes, an hour. Till there's somebody else."

On her first jump, the surface seemed spongy. She stumbled to her knees.

She jumped again. Keeping her knees straight, she went higher.

She leapt again, rising high above the trampoline, above the rides, the grim-faced man on the roller coaster, the giggling girls with their head scarves fluttering above the roller coaster, the pale children in wheelchairs, the painted lady and made-up girl. She jumped, gripping the elastic ropes, as if she could rocket through the glass ceiling, through the rain, beyond gravity.

She landed lightly, and her spring tossed her into the air. At her apex, the storm pulled down a power line a half-mile away, plunging the Old South, the Wild West, the Great Plains and the rest of ersatz America into darkness. Emergency lights freckled on. Some rides stopped cold; gravity defeated the rest. Yelps and squeaks and curses and fear and comforting rose.

Cameras captured one last round of screams and arms, the grim man, the scarved girls, the Pink Duo, rows of empty seats, then blinked into darkness.

At that moment, she thought of riding the roller coaster as a child, gripping the safety bar.

And although it was not the same thing at all, she raised her hands above her head and soared.

Our Contributors

Kristine Rae Anderson's poetry has appeared in *About Place Journal, Copperfield Review, Soundings East,* and *Reed,* among other publications. Her chapbook *Field of Everlasting* is forthcoming in summer 2022 from Main Street Rag. She has received Tomales Bay and Fishtrap fellowships as well as first place in the Mary C. Mohr Poetry Contest (*Southern Indiana Review*). Kristine lives in southern California with her family and their three-legged rescue dog. www.kristineraeanderson.com

Robert P. Arthur grew up on the Chesapeake Bay at Silver Beach, Virginia, and received an athletic scholarship to the University of Richmond. He has a BA and MA from University of Richmond and an MFA from the University of Arkansas, where he studied under Miller Williams, Bill Harrison, and Maxine Kumin. He has published over 1500 articles on the arts, 40 books of poetry, fiction and has had 31 of his plays produced. At Wilkes University, he was a writer in low residence in poetry and playwriting.

Watched by crows and friend to salamanders, **Lisa Creech Bledsoe** is a hiker, beekeeper, and writer living in the mountains of Western North Carolina. She is the author of two full-length books of poetry, *Appalachian Ground* (2019), and *Wolf Laundry* (2020). She has had poems in *Dead Mule School of Southern Literature, Chiron Review, Otoliths, Pine Mountain Sand & Gravel,* and *Quartet,* among others. Website: https://appalachianground.com/

Dianne Blomberg, PhD is an author and speaker living in Colorado. She's published in *Feminine Collective, Across the Margin, Button Eye Review, Alpha Female Society, Dove Tales-Abrazos, Volney Road Review, HerStry, Krazines*, and more. Her essays are featured in "Best Of" publications and anthologies, and she has authored two children's books. Her research in personal relationships is cited in *Good Housekeeping, The Wall Street Journal, USA Today, Family Life, Newsday New York, The Denver Post* and more. Currently, Dianne is working on a collection, *Walk Away*, and co-writing a TV-pilot. She makes time to cherish life and eat ice cream.

Ruth Bonapace: A former journalist, I received my MFA in creative writing from Stony Brook University. My work has appeared in *The Southampton Review, The Saturday Evening Post, Thin Air, The New York Times*, and other publications. My debut novel, *The Bulgarian Training Manual*, is scheduled for publication in 2023 by Clash Books. I live in New Jersey.

Jennifer Bryce is from Melbourne, Australia. She spent many years as a secondary school teacher, educational researcher, and musician before devoting herself to writing. She was a founding member of Elwood Writers (elwoodwriters.com) and has her own blog (jenniferbryce.net). She has published short fiction, reviews, and memoir. Her first novel, *Lily Campbell's Secret* was published in 2019.

Emily Butler is the author of *Lucid Dreaming, Waking Life: Unlocking the Power of Your Sleep* (*Toplight Books*) and the poetry chapbook, *Self Talk* (*Plan B Press*). Their work has appeared or is forthcoming in *The Comstock Review, Painted Bride Quarterly, Spoon River Poetry Review, Cape Cod Poetry Review*, and elsewhere. You can find more of their work at https://linktr.ee/emilyfbutler.

Paola Caronni hails from Italy and has been living in Hong Kong for twenty years. She works as a translator, tutor of Italian, Chief Editor for the English blog of *Ciao Magazine* (*ciaomag.com*), and she is very active on the local poetry scene. Paola holds an MFA in Creative Writing (University of Hong Kong) and an MA in English Language and Literature (University of Milan). Her poems have been published in various anthologies and journals. Her first poetry collection, *Uncharted Waters* (2021) is a winner of the Proverse Prize 2020 and the recipient of a grant from the Hong Kong Arts Development Council.

B. Carroll is a librarian from New Jersey who takes photos, crafts incessantly in multiple media, and inflicts book recommendations on innocent bystanders.

William Cass has had over 250 short stories accepted for publication in a variety of literary magazines such as *december*, *Briar Cliff Review*, and *Zone 3*. He was a finalist in short fiction and novella competitions at *Glimmer Train* and *Black Hill Press*, and won contests at *Terrain.org* and *The Examined Life Journal*. He has received a Best Small Fictions nomination, three Pushcart nominations, and his short story collection, *Something Like Hope & Other Stories*, was recently released by *Wising Up Press*. He lives in San Diego, California.

Armed with an MFA from Boston University, **Cynthia Close** plowed her way through several productive careers in the arts including instructor in drawing and painting, Dean of Admissions at The Art Institute of Boston, founder of ARTWORKS Consulting, and president of Documentary Educational Resources—a nonprofit film distribution company. She now claims to be a writer.

Jean Colonomos began her career in the arts first as a ballerina-in-training at the Old Met and then as a member of the Martha Graham Dance Company. She segued into dance journalism while writing poetry and plays. She has won awards in all three disciplines. Most recently, Ms. Colonomos was a nominee for a Pushcart prize. Thank you, San Fedele Press, for publishing my poems. For more, see jeancolonomos.weebly.com

"Sometimes you need a story more than food to stay alive," says Badger in Barry Lopez's *Crow and Weasel*. **Ruth Ann Dandrea** spent thirty years teaching high school kids to believe this truth. Her stories and poems and essays have appeared in literary magazines, newspapers and education publications. She is co-author of a book on women's kayaking, *WOW: Women on Water*, which was named the *Adirondack Center for Writing's* nonfiction book of 2012. Summer Thursdays you can find her paddling a yellow boat on quiet Adirondack waters.

John Davis is a polio survivor and the author of *Gigs* and *The Reservist*. His work has appeared recently in *DMQ Review*, *Iron Horse Literary Review* and *Terrain.org*

Adam Day is the author of *Left-Handed Wolf* (*LSU Press*, 2020), and *Model of a City in Civil War* (*Sarabande Books*), and the recipient of a Poetry Society of America Chapbook Fellowship for *Badger, Apocryph*a, and of a PEN America Literary Award. He is the publisher of the *cultural magazine*, *Action*, and *Spectacle*.

Lisa Delan is a soprano specializing in American Art Song: performing, recording, and commissioning musical settings of an expansive range of poetry. She has recorded extensively for the Pentatone label and can be heard on Apple Music, Spotify, YouTube, and other streaming platforms. Her poetry appears in *Beyond Words Literary Magazine, Mill Valley Literary Review, Wingless Dreamer, Viewless Wings, Tangled Locks, Cathexis Northwest Press, Lone Mountain Literary Society, The Pointed Circle, Drunk Monkeys*, and *Poets Choice*.

Amy Dupcak: The author of the story collection *Dust* (2016) and co-editor of *Words After Dark* (2020), my work has been published in *Sonora Review, Entropy, Phoebe, Fringe, Litro, Hypertext, Bookanista*, and others. I earned an MFA in Fiction from The New School and studied poetry at Sarah Lawrence College. Currently, I am a writing instructor for adolescents at Writopia Lab and for adults at The Writer's Rock, and Fiction Editor of *Cagibi*.

Patricia Dutt: I am a landscape estimator living in Ithaca, New York. I've published two books and about a dozen short stories in small literary magazines. Almost every day, before work, I am up at the wee hours of the morning, writing.

Jean Ende is a former newspaper reporter, NYC government publicist, corporate marketing executive, and college professor. She has been writing short stories for the past ten years, many based on her immigrant Jewish family. Jean's stories have been published and recognized in over a dozen print and online magazines and literary competitions. She recently completed her first novel and is looking for an agent or publisher.

Jeffrey Feingold is a writer in Boston. His work appears in magazines, such as the international *Intrepid Times*, and *The Bark* (a national magazine with readership over 250,000. Jeffrey's work has also been published by award-winning literary reviews and journals, including *The Pinch, Wilderness House Literary Review, Hare's Paw Literary Journal, Schyulkill Valley Journal, The Raven'sPerch, PAST TEN, The Wise Owl*, and *elsewhere*. Jeffrey's stories about family, about the push-pull of heritage versus assimilation, and about love, loss, regret and forgiveness, reveal a sense of absurdity tempered by a love of people and their quirky ways.

D Ferrara is a writer, editor, and collaborator who considers her role with *American Writers Review* to be an honor and a privilege.

Patricia Florio earned an MFA in creative writing and then after many years in publishing has extended to visual arts. Her folk art style paintings have been included in several shows and her work is moving towards other visual expressions. She is convinced that it is never too late to venture out and experience new genres and venues.

Lara Frankena is a Midwesterner by birth and a Londoner by chance. Her poems have appeared in *Free State Review, Shot Glass Journal, Literary Mama,* and *American Writers Review*.

Christine Gelineau is the author of three full-length books of poetry: *Crave* from NYQ Books; the book-length sequence *Appetite For The Divine*, published as the Editor's Choice for the Robert McGovern Prize from Ashland Poetry Press and *Remorseless Loyalty*, winner of the Richard Snyder Memorial Prize, also from Ashland. A recipient of the Pushcart Prize, Gelineau's poetry, essays, and reviews have appeared widely. Gelineau lives on a farm in New York State and teaches in the Maslow Family Graduate Creative Writing Program at Wilkes University.

Paula Goldman's book, *The Great Canopy*, won the Gival Press Poetry award, and honorable mention for the Independent Booksellers' Award. Her work has appeared in *The Harvard Review, The North American Review, Poet Lore, Hawaii Pacific Review, Arlington Literary Journal, Cæsura*, and others. She won first prize in INKWELL's poetry competition and the Louisiana Literature Award. She holds an MA in Journalism from Marquette and an MFA in Writing from Vermont College. Her newest book is *Late Love* (Kelsay Books 2020. She lives in Milwaukee, WI, with her husband.

Flo Golod's short fiction has appeared in two issues of *Talking Stick* (one received a second-place award), the 2018 *Choices* anthology from Temptation Press, the online journals, *Manifestations, BoomerLit.com*, and in the Darkhouse Press anthology *What We Talk About When We Talk About It: Vol. 1* and *2*. She was accepted into the Tucson Writers Festival Workshop in 2019. She has also published several reflections and opinion pieces that have appeared in a local paper and national blog. She lives, writes, and gardens in Minneapolis.

Jan Elaine Harris' chapbook, *Isolating One's Priorities*, was published by Finishing Line Press in November 2021. Recent poems have appeared, in *Yes, Poetry, The West Trade Review, HERWords, The Portland Review*, etc. Jan is an Associate Professor of Writing at Lipscomb University in Nashville, TN. She lives in East Nashville with her partner and her two perfect GSPs, Malloy and Astrid-June.

Natalie Harrison lives in Sacramento, California, with her husband and daughter. She has a certificate in creative writing from UC Berkeley Extension. Follow her on Twitter @nattywritergirl, Instagram @nattything and listen to all her writing playlists on Spotify @TrillGirl

Janet Ruth Heller is president of the Michigan College English Association. She has published four poetry books: *Nature's Olympics* (Wipf and Stock, 2021), *Exodus* (WordTech Editions, 2014), *Folk Concert: Changing Times* (Anaphora Literary Press, 2012), and *Traffic Stop* (Finishing Line Press, 2011). *The University of Missouri Press* published her scholarly book, *Coleridge, Lamb, Hazlitt, and the Reader of Drama* (1990). Fictive Press published Heller's middle-grade chapter book about sibling rivalry, *The Passover Surprise* (2015, 2016). Her children's book about bullying, *How the Moon Regained Her Shape* (Arbordale, 2006; 6th ed. 2018), has won four national awards. Her website is https://www.janetruthheller.com

Lorraine Jeffery has a Master's degree in library science, and has managed libraries in several states. She has won poetry prizes in state and national contests and published over one hundred poems in journals and anthologies, including *Clockhouse, Kindred, Ibbetson Street, Rockhurst Review, Orchard Street Press, Bacopa Press, Two Hawks, Riverfeet,* and *Naugatuck River Review.* Her work has appeared in many publications, including *Persimmon Tree, Focus on the Family, Elsewhere* and in *Utah Anthologies.* Her first book titled, *When the Universe Brings Us Back*, was published in 2022. She lives in Utah with her husband.

W. Luther Jett: I am a native of Montgomery County, Maryland. My poetry has been published in numerous journals, *including Beltway Poetry Quarterly, Evening Street, Steam Ticket, Potomac Review, Little Patuxent Review,* and *Main Street Rag.*, as well as in *Secrets & Dreams,* Kind of a Hurricane Press; *My Cruel Invention*, Meerkat Press; and *Written in Arlington*, Paycock Press. I am the author of: *Not Quite: Poems Written in Search of My Father*, (Finishing Line Press, 2015), and *Our*

Situation, (Prolific Press, 2018), *Everyone Disappears* (Finishing Line Press, 2020), and *Little Wars* (Kelsay Books, 2021).

Thomas Penn Johnson was born August 22, 1943 in Greensboro, North Carolina. In 1966 he received a BA in Classical Studies from then-Concordia Senior College in Fort Wayne, Indiana. In 1967 he briefly attended Concordia Seminary in Clayton, Missouri, and in 1968 he received an MA in English from UNC-G. He also pursued graduate studies in English literature and history at Syracuse and Wake Forest Universities. In 2009 he retired from then-Edison State College in Fort Myers, Florida, after serving for 26 years as an instructor of English and humanities.

After spending many happy years teaching elementary and middle school students, **Kimberly Behre Kenna** returned to school for her MA in creative writing from Wilkes University. Her debut middle-grade novel, *Artemis Sparke & the Sound Seekers Brigade*, will be published by Regal House/Fitzroy Books on 2/2/23. Her poems and short stories have been published in *American Writers Review*, *Mused*, *Plumtree Tavern*, and *Rubbertop Review*. Kimberly lives on the Connecticut shoreline where she was born and raised and continues to enjoy exploring the waters and beaches of Long Island Sound. Visit her at kimberlybehrekenna.com

Tricia Knoll is a Vermont poet whose work frequently leans into eco-poetry. Recent publications include *Kenyon Review*, *Verse Virtual*, and *The Poeming Pigeon*. Her work is collected in five books—the most recent is *Let's Hear It for the Horses* (3rd places winner of The Poetry Box 2021 chapbook contest) and *Checkered Mates* (Kelsay Books, 2021.) She has two new collections coming out in 2023, one of which is devoted to poetry about trees. Knoll is a Contributing Editor to *Verse Virtual*. Website: triciaknoll.com

Sheree La Puma is an award-winning writer whose work has appeared in *The Penn Review*, *Redivider*, *The Maine Review*, *Rust + Moth*,

The Rumpus, and *Catamaran Literary Reader*, among others. She earned her MFA in writing from CalArts. Her poetry has been nominated for Best of The Net and the Pushcart. She has a new chapbook, *'Broken: Do Not Use.'* (*Main Street Rag Publishing*) www.shereelapuma.com

John Laue, teacher/counselor, a former editor of *Transfer, San Francisco Review*, and *Monterey Poetry Review*, has won the Ina Coolbrith Poetry Prize at The University of California, Berkeley. With six published books including *A Confluence of Voices Revisited* (Futurecycle Press) the most recent. A recognized photographer, Laue has mounted shows of his photos and has had many selected for inclusion in local, national, and international galleries and magazines.

Jonathan Lawrence is a poet from Bethlehem, Pennsylvania. He currently teaches tenth grade English and Creative Writing and is a student in the Maslow Family Graduate Program in Creative Writing at Wilkes University. His poetry review has been published in *Newfound*.

Miriam Levine is the author of *Saving Daylight*, her fifth collection of poetry. Another collection, *The Dark Opens*, was chosen by Mark Doty for the Autumn House Poetry Prize. Other books include: *Devotion, a* memoir; *In Paterson*, a novel. Her work has appeared in *American Poetry Review*, *The Kenyon Review*, *The Paris Review*, and *Ploughshares*. Levine, a fellow of the NEA and a grantee of the Massachusetts Artists Foundation, lives in Florida and New Hampshire. For more information about her work, please go to miriamlevine.com.

C.L. Liedekev is a poet/propagandist who lives in Conshohocken, PA with his real name, wife, and children. He attended most of his life in the Southern part of New Jersey. His work has been published in such places *as Humana Obscura, Red Fez, MacQueen's, Hare's Paw, River Heron Review*, amongst others. His poem, "November Snow. Philadelphia Children's Hospital," is a finalist for the 2021 Best of the Net.

Robin Long is a queer poet and writer in Austin. She's expanding her original fiction thesis on the life of Emily Dickinson, *The Other Dickinson*, and found at theotherdickinson.com. Robin was a 2020 Pushcart Prize nominee and National Poetry Month Editor's Pick for Brain Mill Press; a performer in the FEELS+Artery LIVE Digital Poetry Event series; and a First Line Poetry Series finalist with *Alexandria Quarterly*. Her poetry is found in *FEELS Zine, Art in the Time of Covid-19*, and the *2021 Texas Poetry Calendar*, among others.

George Looney's books are *The Visibility of Things Long Submerged*, winner, BOA Editions Short Fiction Award, *Ode to the Earth in Translation*, *The Worst May Be Over*, winner, Elixir Press Fiction Award, *The Itinerate Circus: New and Selected Poems 1995-2020*, the Red Mountain Press Poetry Award-winning *What Light Becomes*, and *Report from a Place of Burning,* co-winner of Leapfrog Press Fiction Award. He founded the BFA in Creative Writing Program, Penn State Erie, editor-in-chief of literary journal *Lake Effect*, translation editor of *Mid-American Review*, and co-founder of the original Chautauqua Writers' Festival.

Carol MacAllister is a widely published poet, author, and exhibiting artist. She holds an MFA in Creative Writing with a concentration in Fiction and Poetry, an MA in Creative Non-Fiction and an MFA in Fine Arts. She has judged the National Federation of State Poetry Societies' competitions and has produced *RIPASSO,* a limited-edition collection of poetry by well-known poet laurates and poets, including Robert Pinsky. MacAllister has edited and produced several collections, and is published with Northampton House Press.

Nancy Matsunaga is a freelance writer and teacher who lives with her family in the New York area. She is affiliated with The Writers Studio, a creative writing school based in New York, where she has taught live and online classes since 2007. Her work has appeared in the journal *Calyx* and was anthologized in *The Writers Studio* at 30. She was a finalist for the Chester B. Himes Memorial Short Fiction prize and a nominee for the Pushcart Prize.

Mona Deutsch Miller, writer since childhood, has had 10 plays produced in Southern California. She also writes short stories, essays, screenplays and poetry that she rarely shows to anyone. Productions include the one-hour absurdist play, *The Beating*, about jurors' perceptions of a criminal trial, short comedies Receipts, *The End of the Line* (published under the title *Strangers on a Train*), and *Rock Around the Campfire* (about peace in the Middle East). Her short play about homelessness, *Sardines*, is included in Lawrence Harbison's Best New 10-Minute Plays of 2020. "My Father" is her first published poem in a very long time.

Pam Munter has authored several books including *When Teens Were Keen: Freddie Stewart and The Teen Agers of Monogram, Almost Famous*, and *As Alone As I Want To Be*. She's a former clinical psychologist, performer, and film historian. Her essays, book reviews, and short stories have appeared in more than 200 publications. Her play, *Life Without* was nominated by the Desert Theatre League. She has been nominated for a Pushcart Prize, and is a winner of the Sara Patton Award. *Fading Fame: Women of a Certain Age in Hollywood* was published in 2021. Her work can be found at www.pammunter.com.

J. Alan Nelson, a writer and actor, has essays, stories and poetry published or forthcoming in journals including *New York Quarterly, Conjunctions, Stand, Acumen, Pampelmousse, Main Street Rag, Texas Observer, California Quarterly, Connecticut River Review, Adirondack Review, Red Cedar Review, Wisconsin Review, South Carolina Review, Kairos, Ligeia, Strange Horizons, Illuminations, Review Americana* and *Whale Road Review*. He has received nominations for Best of Net and Best Microfiction.

Don Noel, retired from four decades' prizewinning print and broadcast journalism in Hartford CT, took his MFA in Creative Writing from Fairfield University in 2013, and has published more than five dozen short stories, which can be read at his website, https://dononoel.com

Jill Ocone is a senior writer and editor for *Jersey Shore Magazine* and Jersey Shore Publications' annual guidebooks. Her work has also been published in Read Furiously's anthology *Stay Salty: Life in the Garden State*; Exeter Publishing's *From the Soil* hometown anthology; Red Penguin Books' *Where Flowers Bloom, the leaves fall and 'Tis the Season: Poems for Your Holiday Spirit*; and *American Writers Review*, among others. A 22-year high school journalism educator, Jill squeezes as much out of life as possible and loves making memories with her nieces and nephews. Visit Jill at jillocone.com.

Mary K O'Melveny, a retired labor lawyer, lives with her wife in Woodstock, NY, and Washington DC. Mary has received a Pushcart Prize nomination and awards in national and international poetry contests. Her poetry appears in many journals, anthologies, and national blogs such as *The New Verse News*. She is the author of *A Woman of a Certain Age*, *Merging Star Hypotheses* (Finishing Line Press 2018, 2020) and *Dispatches from The Memory Care Museum* (Kelsay Books 2021) and co-author of: *An Apple In Her Hand* (Codhill Press 2019) and *Rethinking The Ground Rules* (Mediacs Books 2022).

Esther Lim Palmer is the author of two chapbooks, *Stellar* (*Finishing Line Press*, 2021) and *Janus* (*Finishing Line Press*, 2020). Her work has appeared in various literary journals and anthologies, including *California Quarterly, Plainsongs, White Wall Review, Westwind, Poetry in the Time of Coronavirus, Volume 2, The Hungry Chimera, Brief Wilderness*, and Oberon's Seventeenth Annual Issue—selected to be archived in the EBSCO's Humanities of contemporary literary work. She currently lives and writes in San Francisco.

Mandy Pennington is a digital marketer, teacher, writer and student in the Maslow Family Graduate Program in Creative Writing at Wilkes University. Published in the *Northeastern Pennsylvania Business Journal*, **White**, and Boston.com's *The Next Great Generation,* she lives in Scranton with her husband and two mischievous cats.

Cindy Pope is an award-winning author who has written for magazines such as *Enjoy Cherokee* and *Birmingham*, and trade magazines like *The Independent Restauranteur* and *Business Alabama Monthly.* Her short stories have won awards, and her blogs can be seen on Pink Fuzzy Slippers.com and The-Write-One.com. When not interviewing local movers and shakers for *Enjoy Cherokee* magazine, Cindy stays busy researching and writing works of fiction and creative non-fiction. Cindy is currently a graduate student in the Master of Arts Professional Writing program at Kennesaw State University.

Carol Radsprecher's images earned her MFA in painting in 1988 from Hunter College, CUNY. A longtime painter, she discovered the wonders of digital image-making and found that media well suited to her need to make a succession of rapidly-evolving narrative images based on distorted representations of the human body, especially the female body. Her work has appeared in several solo shows and numerous group shows and has been published in print and/or online publications. Her website is https://www.carolradsprecher.com.

Burt Rashbaum's publications are *Of the Carousel* (The Poet's Press, 2019), and *Blue Pedals* (Editura Pim, 2015, Bucharest). His poems have been anthologized in *XY Files* (Sherman Asher Publishing, 1997), *The Cento* (Red Hen Press, 2011), *Art in the Time of Covid-19* (San Fedele Press, 2020), *A 21st Century Plague: Poetry from a Pandemic* (University Professors Press, 2021*), American Writers Review: Turmoil and Recovery* (San Fedele Press, 2021), and most recently, *The Antonym*. His recent fiction has appeared in *Meet Cute Press*, *Caesura*, and *Typeslash Review*, and the 2022 spring/summer issue of *Collateral*.

Christina Reiss has been a finalist or semi-finalist in the Scribes Publishing, Howard Frank Mosher, Able Muse, Tiferet, Kallisto Gaia Press, San Fedele Press's American Writers in Review, and Great Midwest Writing short story contests and an honorable mention for the Hat Prize. She has published short stories in *Fail Better, Scarlett Leaf, Pulse Peninsula, Scribes Anthology*, and *Watershed* and will publish additional work in *Midway Journal* this summer. She lives in Vermont, works in the judiciary, is the mother of three daughters, and is married to a woodworker.

Pat Ryan's short fiction has appeared *in American Writers Review, Chautauqua: Boundaries* and *Chautauqua*: *Moxie issues*; *The Ghost Story*; and *The Hopper*. Her reviews and articles on movies, music, and literature have appeared in numerous publications, including *The New York Times*, where she was an editor in the Culture Department. Her story "Say Hello to Pudgy," is part of a collection of linked stories. She lives and writes in Deerfield, Mass, where she is a member of the Cultural Council.

Terry Sanville lives in San Luis Obispo, California with his artist-poet wife (his in-house editor) and two plump cats (his in-house critics). He writes full time, producing short stories, essays, and novels. His short stories have been accepted more than 490 times by journals, magazines, and anthologies including *The Potomac Review, The Bryant Literary Review*, and *Shenandoah*. He was nominated twice for Pushcart Prizes and once for inclusion in Best of the Net anthology. Terry is a retired urban planner and an accomplished jazz and blues guitarist –who once played with a symphony orchestra backing up jazz legend George Shearing.

Joel Savishinsky is an anthropologist and gerontologist: his books include *The Trail of the Hare: Life and Stress in an Arctic Community*, and *Breaking The Watch: The Meanings of Retirement in America*, which won the Gerontological Society of America's Kalish Award, a book-of-the-year prize. His poetry, fiction and nonfiction have appeared in *American Writers Review, Beyond Words, Blood and Thunder, Cirque, The Examined Life Journal, The New York Times, Poetry Quarterly, SLANT, Toho Journal*, and *Windfall*. He lives in Seattle, helping to raise grandchildren, a recovering academic and unrepentant activist. savishin@gmail.com

Patty Somlo's most recent book, *Hairway to Heaven Stories* (Cherry Castle Publishing), was a Finalist in the American Fiction Awards and Best Book Awards. Two previous books, *The First to Disappear* (Spuyten Duyvil) and *Even When Trapped Behind Clouds: A Memoir of Quiet Grace* (WiDo Publishing), were Finalists in several book contests. Her work has appeared in numerous journals and over 30 anthologies. She received Honorable Mention for Fiction in the Women's National Book Association Contest, was a Finalist in the Parks and Points Essay Contest, and had an essay selected as Notable for Best American Essays.

Ana Fores Tamayo: An underpaid academic, I wanted to do something that mattered: work with asylum seekers. I advocate for marginalized refugee families from Mexico and Central America. Working with asylum seekers is heart wrenching, satisfying, and humbling. My labor has eased my sense of displacement, being a child refugee. I have published in The Raving Press, Indolent Books, Laurel Review, Shenandoah, and other anthologies and journals, in the US and internationally. My poetry and accompanying photography has been exhibited in art fairs and galleries. The manuscript Peregrina, will be published by Ediciones Valparaiso.

Holly Tappen is a writer and artist in Minneapolis. She specializes in Post-Depressionism.

Barry Lee Thompson's short stories are published in Australia, the UK, and the USA, and recognised in awards including the Bridport Prize and the Overland Victoria University Short Story Prize. *Broken Rules and Other Stories*, his first book, is published by Transit Lounge. Barry is developing a second collection, supported by the Victorian Government through Creative Victoria and Regional Arts Victoria. He is a member of the Alumni Association of Varuna, the National Writers' House, and is a founding member of Elwood Writers. Visit barryleethompson.com.

G.R. Tomaini is author of five books of poetry and one philosophical encyclopedia; three of his books of poetry are due to be published soon and so too is his encyclopedia. Tomaini is also the student of Dr. Cornel West at Union Theological Seminary. His work can be found at grtomaini.com.

Bissera Videnova is a Bulgarian-born poet, writer, editor, and translator in her native tongue. She has a poetry collection in her country, translated works in English, French, Italian, Korean, Romanian; Holds a prize for prose—France (2012); participates in poetry readings at the Poetry House in New York and the Yale Royal Poetry Club in Manhattan (2014-2019).

Tommy Vollman is a writer, musician, and painter, and once, a baseball player. He has written a number of things, published a bit, recorded a few records, and toured a lot. His stories and nonfiction have appeared in *The Southwest Review, Two Cities Review, Hobart, The Southeast Review, Palaver*, and *Per Contra*. He has black-ink tattoos on his arms. Tommy likes A. Moonlight Graham, Kurt Vonnegut, Two Cow Garage, Tillie Olsen, Willy Vlautin, and Albert Camus. He's working on a short story collection and has a new record, *Youth or Something Beautiful*.

Tim Walker read, for pleasure, the novels of Charles Dickens while earning a BA in Environmental Studies, and the novels of Anthony Trollope while earning a PhD in Geological Sciences, and has since worked as a computer programmer, healthcare data analyst, used book seller, and pet sitter. He lives largely in his own head, while he corporeally resides in Santa Barbara with his son and their cat. His essays and poems have appeared or are forthcoming in *Entropy Magazine, Ragazine, Squalorly, DIAGRAM, pacificREVIEW, Coastal Shelf,* and *Rat's Ass Review.*

Kresha Richman Warnock retired, with her husband, to the Pacific Northwest right before the pandemic hit. The timing seemed right to begin writing seriously. She is working on her memoir and shorter essays, trying to focus on nuance in the hard questions of the day and look at the humanity of each of us. Returning to the area where she grew up, after living around the US for many years, has rekindled in her a desire to tell some of the stories she lived going back to the 1960s. She is the mother of two grown children and grandmother to two granddogs.

Marian Willmott :I am an artist and writer, enjoying both the solitude of the Vermont mountains and a vital artistic community. Although I have always loved to write, I was primarily a visual artist until shortly after my mother died and I was moved to begin writing more seriously. I now enjoy the balance and interaction of both forms of expression. My work has been published in many literary journals and two poetry chapbooks: *Turnings*, published by Pudding House Publications in 2007 and *Still Life, Requiem and an Egg*, published by Prolific Press in 2018.

Edward Wilson's poems have appeared in *The American Poetry Review, Beloit Poetry Journal, The Georgia Review, The Midwest Quarterly, Poetry (Chicago), The Southern Poetry Review, The South Carolina Review*, and others. His awards include an Individual Artist Fellowship from the state of Georgia, a Bread Loaf Writers' Conference Fellowship and an NEA Fellowship. His collection, *In a Rich Country,* won the Grayson Books Poetry Prize and was selected as a finalist in the 2020 Georgia Author of the Year Awards. He lives in Augusta, Georgia.

Kris Whorton, originally from Boulder, teaches writing at the University of Tennessee and the Hamilton and Bradley County Jails. She teaches teens and works with adults in the mental health sector. Her poetry has appeared in *The Greensboro Review* #109, *Wild Roof Journal* and *Salmon Creek Journal,* and her fiction in *Driftwood Press, Scarlet Leaf Review*, and elsewhere; she was a guest editor for *Roots Rated,* and her creative nonfiction has been featured in *Get Out magazine.*

San Fedele Press

"Truth is stranger than fiction, but it is because Fiction is obliged to stick to possibilities; Truth isn't."

- Mark Twain

San Fedele Press

About Us

American Writers Review is a multi-genre literary journal published by San Fedele Press. We welcome writers, artists, and photographers of all backgrounds, styles and experience levels, who want to explore their art with us.

www.AmericanWritersReview.com

Made in United States
North Haven, CT
28 July 2022

21952689R00168